MALTESE

Printed and Distributed by T.F.H. Publications, Inc.
Neptune City, NJ

MALTESE

Kathy DiGiacomo & Barbara J. Bergquist

T.F.H. Publications, Inc.
One TFH Plaza
Third and Union Avenues
Neptune City, NJ 07753

This book has been published with the intent to provide accurate and authoritative information in regard to the subject matter within. While every precaution has been taken in preparation of this book, the publisher and author assume no responsibility for errors or omissions. Neither is any liability assumed for damages resulting from the use of the information herein.

ISBN 0-7938-2384-6

Printed and bound in the United States of America

www.tfh.com

About This Book

Maltese is an updated version of the best-selling, breed-specific series from T. F. H. Publications. This modernized edition of the popular guide contains the most recent information available about the breed, from its history and origins to training techniques, as well as tips on selecting the right dog for you, grooming, feeding, obedience training, exercise, and health care. Complemented by all-new photographs, each book in the series provides purebred dog owners with all the advice they will need to raise a happy, healthy dog.

Other T.F.H. Books available on the Maltese:

A New Owner's Guide to Maltese
Vicki Abbott

The Guide to Owning a Maltese
Brandlyn James

The Maltese
Anna Katherine Nicholas

Contents

His small stature and adorable appearance make the Maltese a favorite among dog fanciers.

History and Development of the Maltese

The Maltese is a beautiful little toy dog. Members of the breed are alert, intelligent, loyal, and sensitive, but above all, they are extremely loving. In return, Maltese owners have love and deep respect for the breed.

Maltese make excellent house pets because they are easily trained and are clean animals. Although they require grooming to maintain the brightness and fine texture of their coat, they seem to enjoy this procedure—perhaps another example of their desire for attention and companionship with human members of the family.

Maltese develop with good speed and generally mature mentally before their first birthday.

The Maltese enjoys great popularity for his marvelous ways and steady disposition.

EARLY BACKGROUND

Despite the fact that the name "Maltese" has been used for thousands of years, there is some mystery concerning the actual beginning of the breed of dog that is now recognized as the Maltese. Several theories have been advanced to explain the evolvement from a body type that some people first thought to be a spaniel-type structure, but that was later considered to be more of a terrier-type. Even fairly modern kennel club records described the Maltese as being spaniels (not terriers), while at the same time they sometimes referred to them as Maltese Terriers.

Perhaps the matter has best been resolved by present usage, which is simply to call the breed by the name Maltese and not worry about whether it actually began on the island of Malta or if the little dogs of ancient Egyptians were or were not similar to those of today.

MALTESE AROUND THE WORLD

Although known in Great Britain much earlier, it can be verified that the Maltese has been bred and shown in England since the late 1800s. The breed is still popular there, with a Maltese winning the Toy Group at Crufts in 1983.

Among the English kennels are Invicta, Harlingen, Rhosneigh, Leckhampton, Yelwa, and Ellwin. The Vicbrita Kennels are the most

Through selective breeding, different types of dogs came to have different duties. Some breeds, like the Maltese, had the sole purpose of being companion dogs.

As delicate as a porcelain figurine, the Maltese has captured the hearts of owners in homes around the world.

well known, as they have bred many English champions and have also exported dogs that have become American champions and producers of champions. The Gissing Kennels were originally in England before moving to Portugal. The Suirside Kennels are located in Ireland.

English and American Maltese are not identical; the American version is quite often finer boned and smaller, with a shorter muzzle and different coat texture. As more English and American Maltese are bred together, the chance of greater similarity will, of course, increase.

The Maltese is extremely popular in Canada. Many American dogs are shown in Canada, and vice versa, as the bloodlines are very similar.

Italy is also known for quality Maltese. Dr. Vincenzo Calvaresi (Villa Malta) imported many dogs from the Electa Kennels and helped develop a different line in the US. Perhaps the interest in the Maltese on the part of Italian owners and breeders is a reflection of a time when these dogs appeared in artwork of the Renaissance period. There are also the legends of small dogs from Melita, an ancient town in Sicily, from which, these stories say, the Maltese may have developed.

The Maltese currently is one of the most popular of all breeds in Japan, and as many as 300 Maltese have appeared at one specialty show. Some of the top dogs and top bloodlines from the US have been sold to Japanese owners, furthering the exceptionally fine specimens of Maltese seen in Japan.

These Maltese pups have a lot of personality in a small package.

The Maltese is an intelligent and intuitive toy dog of fine regal bearing.

MALTESE IN THE US

The American Kennel Club officially opened its stud book for Maltese in 1888. The Maltese was first entered in shows within the Miscellaneous Class, then moved to the Non-Sporting Group, and finally settled into the Toy Group.

The breed has been very fortunate to have had many truly dedicated breeders and fanciers right from the beginning. There is a great future for this beautiful breed as Maltese dogs continue to improve in type, soundness, and condition every year.

For many Americans, the first recollection of a Maltese was when Dr. Calvaresi showed his brace and team at Westminster in the 1950s. It was an event that is still talked about and that firmly established the breed in the US. Naturally, the Villa Malta line became established first. Nearly every one of today's Maltese has some Villa Malta bloodlines behind it, as many of the top kennels based their breeding programs on Villa Malta dogs.

Mrs. Virginia T. Leitch (Jon Vir) purchased stock from Villa Malta Kennels in England and Ireland and blended these lines very successfully. Mrs. Leitch is respected and remembered by all Maltese fanciers for her history of the breed, *The Maltese Dog*, published in 1953 and now a collector's item.

The American Maltese Association (parent club for the breed in the US) now has more than 500 members. Among the founders of that association are Mr. and Mrs. J.P. Antonelli (Aennchen's Dancers) of New Jersey, Mr. and Mrs. Robert Craig (Goodtime) of Illinois, and Dr. Helen Schively-Poggi (Reveille) of California. These dedicated breeders also had time to breed dogs that have stamped their mark on the Maltese as a breed. If it were not for their hard work, fanciers might not even recognize the marvelous breed as it is today.

A Description of the Maltese

A breed standard is the criterion by which the appearance (and, to a certain extent, the temperament) of any given dog is evaluated. Basically, the standard for any breed is a definition of the perfect specimen, to which all members of the breed may be compared. The degree of excellence of the dog, therefore, is in direct proportion to how well that dog meets the stated requirements for its breed.

Breed standards vary from country to country and from registry to registry. Become familiar with the standard that applies to your area.

The Maltese's drop ears are rather low set and heavily feathered with long hair that hangs close to the head.

Even the most perfect specimen of the breed will fall short of the standard in some respect. It is virtually impossible for any dog to receive unanimous acclaim by everyone who compares it to the standard and to other dogs of the same breed, because a certain amount of subjective evaluation is involved in the interpretation of the wording of the standard—and because even dog judges are human.

Typically, a breed standard is drawn up by a national breed club (known as the parent club for that breed) and approved by a national kennel club, which is the governing body for purebred dogs in a particular country or geographical region. Any such standard is always subject to change through review by the clubs involved.

Official standards for the Maltese have been approved by several of the registering kennel clubs. For the most part, the requirements are essentially the same in those standards; however, even minor differences must be taken into consideration if a dog is to be shown under different jurisdictions. Any Maltese owner is advised to obtain a copy of the most recent standard approved by the kennel club under which the dog is registered, and also to keep up with current information regarding possible revisions in that standard.

A Description of the Maltese

The head of the Maltese should be of medium length and in proportion to the body.

For your convenience, as well as for comparison purposes, we are presenting in this book the standards for the Maltese as approved by the American Kennel Club and The Kennel Club (England).

AMERICAN KENNEL CLUB STANDARD FOR THE MALTESE

General Appearance—The Maltese is a toy dog covered from head to foot with a mantle of long, silky, white hair. He is gentle-mannered and affectionate, eager and sprightly in action, and, despite his size, possessed of the vigor needed for the satisfactory companion.

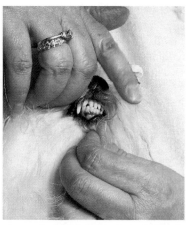

As per the breed standard, the Maltese's teeth meet in an even, edge-to-edge bite or in a scissors bite.

Head—Of medium length and in proportion to the size of the dog. **The skull** is slightly rounded on top, the stop moderate. **The drop ears** are rather low set and heavily feathered with long hair that hangs close to the head. **Eyes** are set not too far apart; they are very dark and round, their black rims enhancing the gentle yet alert expression. **The muzzle** is of medium length, fine and tapered but not snipy. **The nose** is black. **The teeth** meet in an even, edge-to-edge bite, or in a scissors bite.

Neck—Sufficient length of neck is desirable as promoting a high carriage of the head.

Body—Compact, the height from the withers to the ground equaling the length from the withers to the root of the tail. Shoulder blades are sloping, the elbows well knit and held close to the body. The back is

According to the breed standard, the Maltese's eyes are set not too far apart. They are very dark and round, with their black rims enhancing the gentle, yet alert, expression.

level in topline, the ribs well sprung. The chest is fairly deep, the loins taut, strong, and just slightly tucked up underneath.

Tail—A long-haired plume carried gracefully over the back, its tip lying to the side over the quarter.

Legs and Feet—Legs are fine-boned and nicely feathered. Forelegs are straight, their pastern joints well knit and devoid of appreciable bend. Hind legs are strong and moderately angulated at stifles and hocks. The feet are small and round, with toe pads black. Scraggly hairs on the feet may be trimmed to give a neater appearance.

Coat and Color—The coat is single, that is, without undercoat. It hangs long, flat, and silky over the sides of the body almost, if not quite, to the ground. The long head-hair may be tied up in a topknot or it may be left hanging. Any suggestion of kinkiness, curliness, or woolly texture is objectionable. Color, pure white. Light tan or lemon on the ears is permissible, but not desirable.

Size—Weight under 7 pounds, with from 4 to 6 pounds preferred. Overall quality is to be favored over size.

Gait—The Maltese moves with a jaunty, smooth, flowing gait.

The Maltese's back should be straight and level and not drop from back to front.

The Maltese is covered from head to foot with a mantle of long, silky, white hair.

These Maltese display the playful, lively temperament that is called for in the breed standard.

Viewed from the side, he gives an impression of rapid movement, size considered. In the stride, the forelegs reach straight and free from the shoulders, with elbows close. Hind legs to move in a straight line. Cowhocks or any suggestion of hind leg toeing in or out are faults.

Temperament—For all his diminutive size, the Maltese seems to be without fear. His trust and affectionate responsiveness are very appealing. He is among the gentlest mannered of all little dogs, yet he is lively and playful as well as vigorous.

Approved March 10, 1964

THE KENNEL CLUB (ENGLAND) STANDARD FOR THE MALTESE

General Appearance—Smart, white-coated dog, with proud head carriage.

Characteristics—Lively, intelligent, alert.

Temperament—Sweet-tempered.

Head and Skull—From stop to centre of skull (centre between forepart of ears) and stop to tip of nose, equally balanced. Stop well defined. Nose black. Muzzle broad, well filled under eye. Not snipy.

Eyes—Oval, not bulging, dark brown, black eye rims, with dark haloes.

Ears—Long, well feathered, hanging close to head; hair to mingle with coat at shoulders.

Mouth—Jaws strong, with perfect, regular and complete scissor bite, i.e. upper teeth closely overlapping lower teeth and set square to the jaws. Teeth even.

Neck—Medium length.

Forequarters—Legs short and straight. Shoulders well sloped.

Body—Well balanced, essentially short and cobby. Good spring of rib, back level from withers to tail.

Hindquarters—Legs short, well angulated.

Feet—Round, pads black.

Tail—Feathered, carried well arched over back.

Gait/Movement—-Straight and free-flowing, without weaving. Viewed from behind, legs should neither be too close nor too wide apart.

Coat—Good length, not impeding action, straight, of silky texture, never woolly. Never crimped and without woolly undercoat.

Colour—Pure white, but slight lemon markings permissible.

The Maltese's gait should be free, straight, and easy all around.

A Description of the Maltese

Your Maltese should be neatly presented: the long, flat, silky coat should hang over the sides, almost touching the ground.

The Maltese is a compact dog with good balance and substance. The ideal weight is four to six pounds.

Size—Height not exceeding 25 cms (10 ins) from ground to withers.

Faults—Any departure from the foregoing points should be considered a fault and the seriousness with which the fault should be regarded should be in exact proportion to its degree.

Note—Male animals should have two apparently normal testicles fully descended into the scrotum.

September 2000

CHAPTER 3

Owning and Caring for the Maltese

The Maltese is a long-coated breed, and you, as owner and friend, must assume the responsibility for the dog's comfort and well-being. This will require time, patience, and love, but you will receive the rewards of a beautiful, clean, well-groomed, and happy little Maltese.

The following information on general care of the Maltese is intended to familiarize you with certain essential needs that apply to

Grooming sessions should begin when your Maltese is still a pup. By beginning while he is young, he will become accustomed to the routine and enjoy being groomed.

In order to groom your Maltese, you need to obtain the proper grooming instruments.

the Maltese in particular. If you have any doubts, fears, or questions about caring for a Maltese, please consult your veterinarian or other appropriate professional.

Despite their obvious smallness, a Maltese is not a sickly, frail creature. Rather, the Maltese is a sturdy, strong little toy dog. It should be remembered that all breeds of dog require basic care. The coat care, however, is unique to the Maltese and just a few other breeds.

A Maltese, especially a puppy, must be checked regularly for any excrement caught in his "pants" or "skirt." If stool catches in the hair and is not noticed, within a few days it may completely block elimination and cause a ruptured anus or even death. The hair can be trimmed away from the anus, but checking this area daily as part of a routine is more desirable. Washing should take place as necessary. The problem will generally not occur if the dog expels firm, healthy stools, indicating good digestion of a proper diet.

Maltese should be thoroughly brushed at least twice weekly. Always brush the coat in the direction that it naturally lies.

If you are uncomfortable with grooming your Maltese, there are professional groomers that can help.

If you notice your Maltese scooting across the floor or sitting on his behind for a prolonged period of time, he has a problem that requires immediate attention. Either he has stool caught in his hair or he is attempting to empty his anal glands, which are located just inside the anal opening. Their function is to secrete a liquid that helps in the process of elimination. These glands sometimes become blocked and must then be emptied by you or your veterinarian. It is wise to ask your vet to show you the proper procedure at first; then you can do it as part of a routine to prevent such blockage of the glands, which is painful and often requires surgery for the removal of the glands.

Sunlight is required for the overall general health of the Maltese, as well as for the intense black pigment that gives these animals such a beautiful expression. Your Maltese will enjoy daily romps outdoors throughout the year, but dry him off on rainy days and remove the "snowballs" he is sure to collect on his long coat during the winter.

GROOMING SUPPLIES

In order to keep your dog looking good, you need to have the right tools. There is a large selection of grooming equipment available for

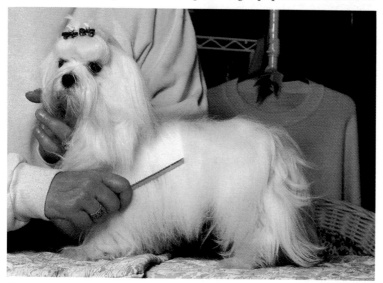

Proper grooming can also help keep your Maltese healthy. Daily brushing will allow you to inspect the dog's coat for fleas, ticks, and other parasites.

every coat type, but there are some universal tools that every owner should have in order to perform general grooming duties.

Here is a list of grooming tools that every dog owner should have:

1. Slicker brush: This versatile brush can work on many different types of coat. The wire bristles grasp and remove a dog's undercoat, help reduce shedding, and keep the coat from becoming matted.

2. Flea comb: A fine-toothed flea comb will be helpful in getting hard-to-reach spots and will remove any flea or flea dirt that may be in your dog's coat.

3. Towels: Old towels are always handy and can be used to wipe off muddy paws and dry off wet coats.

4. Grooming glove: This tool (also called a hound glove) is wonderful for dogs with short coats because it helps loosen any dead hair and gets rid of surface dirt.

5. Nail clippers: Every dog, no matter what coat type, needs to have his nails trimmed. A good pair of canine nail clippers will be very useful if you decide to tackle this task yourself.

6. Doggy toothbrush and toothpaste: Keeping your puppy's teeth clean is essential for maintaining his good health. Be sure to purchase toothpaste and toothbrushes that are especially made for dogs.

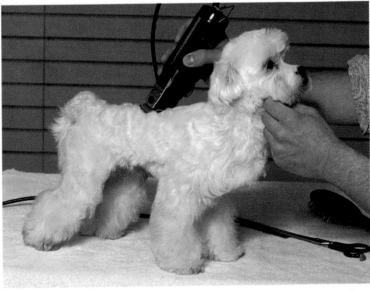

By keeping your Maltese's coat trimmed, you help to keep your pup free from parasites that may spread disease.

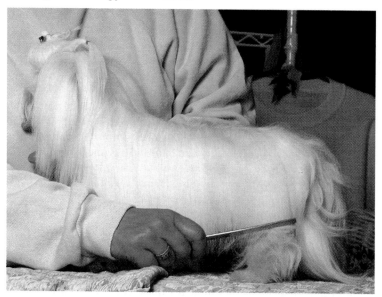

Your Maltese should be thoroughly groomed every other day. Regular sessions will keep your dog looking his best.

Never use human toothpaste when brushing your puppy's teeth. Dogs will not spit out the toothpaste, like humans do, but will swallow it, which can cause stomach upset and digestive problems. Also, the minty taste that humans enjoy probably will not be as appealing to your puppy as it is to you. Canine toothpaste comes in "doggy-friendly" flavors, such as beef and poultry, and is edible.

7. Shampoo: There are many brands of canine shampoo available, as well as ones that have special purposes, such as flea shampoos, medicated shampoos, and whiteners. If you are unsure about what brand to buy, ask your veterinarian for a recommendation.

8. Conditioner: Dogs with long coats may need a conditioner to help remove tangles after bathing. As with shampoos, your vet can recommend a brand that is right for your dog.

9. Scissors: Blunt-nosed scissors are handy for trimming the excess fur on your dog's feet, legs, tail, or anal region, as well as for trimming your dog's whiskers.

GETTING STARTED

Puppyhood is the best time to start grooming procedures, because your dog will more easily become used to the grooming routine and soon come to expect it as part of his everyday life. This is especially true if you have a dog that requires extensive grooming or if you plan to show your puppy when he gets older. It is best to start out slowly so that he doesn't become overwhelmed or frightened, and then build on grooming time until you have the whole routine down pat.

If your puppy requires lots of grooming time, it is best to invest in a good grooming table. While he is getting beautiful, your dog's leash can be attached to the grooming arm on the table, which will help keep him secure. Most tables also have nonskid pads on the surface to keep your dog from sliding around. A grooming table will save your back as well, because it can be adjusted to your height and make it unnecessary for you to bend over or kneel down.

Introduce your puppy to the grooming table slowly. Place him on it without doing anything to him, and give him a treat when you let him down. After you do this a several times, your puppy should eagerly get up on the grooming table. You can then start lightly brushing him and running any appliances like hair dryers or clippers before actually doing anything major to his coat. When he seems totally comfortable, you can start grooming him on a regular basis. This gradual introduction will ensure that your puppy grows to enjoy his grooming time with you. Once your puppy is accustomed to being touched, patted, and fussed over, you can start a grooming routine that will keep him looking clean and healthy.

ROUTINE GROOMING PROCEDURES

A Maltese should be thoroughly groomed every other day (or at least twice a week) to maintain good healthy skin and to promote the long, white, silky coat.

If you obtained your Maltese as a puppy from a concerned and dedicated breeder, that pup most likely has already been trained for what should be an enjoyable, pleasant grooming session. It is up to you to continue this practice, as a dirty and matted Maltese is very unhappy and most uncomfortable. If your puppy was not trained for the grooming procedures, just be patient. In time he will learn to enjoy the sessions.

The question most asked of Maltese breeders is, "How do you get your Maltese to behave so well while you're grooming him?" The answer is, simply, "patience, patience, and more patience." The following routine will aid you in grooming your Maltese. It will also help the experience become a pleasurable one for you and your dog. The time will pass quickly, and before you know it you'll be an

Your Maltese's hair may be put up in a single or double topknot.

Bathe your Maltese only when he is dirty. Excessive bathing will dry out your dog's skin.

expert. The directions may sound complicated at first, but once you get the knack it will only take a few minutes a day.

Begin by training your Maltese to lie still on his back in your lap while running your fingers up and down his tummy and each leg. When he cooperates, praise him. Next, train him to lie on his back on a table covered with a rubber mat so he will not slip. A sink mat is perfect if you do not have a grooming table that already has a non-slip surface.

Comb and brush both tummy and legs in layers. If you notice small mats within the coat, remove

Dry your Maltese's coat thoroughly after bathing him. If it is a nice day, let him finish drying outside.

them by first separating the hairs with your fingers and the end tooth of a comb. Then comb through carefully. Once you have completed the tummy and legs, stand your puppy up (or lay him on first one side and then the other) as you groom each side. First brush in layers, then comb through. Continue with the brushing of chest, tail, skirt or pants, and the area under the tail. For the head, ears, and face, you will use only the comb—being very careful while working around the eyes to avoid any injury.

SINGLE AND DOUBLE TOPKNOTS

If the head hair is long, you can put it up in a single or double topknot. To do this, you will need a small square (a little larger than one inch by one inch) of waxed paper, plastic wrap, or net (nylon tulle). You will also need a rubber band or two.

Part the hair at the outer corners of the eyes and across the top of the head, just in front of the ears. If one topknot is in order, merely pull the hair up and away from the eyes in ponytail fashion. Place the square of material around this section, close to the head. Fold this "package" over once, and then secure it with the rubber band. Do not despair if the results of your first few attempts are less than attractive; practice will make perfect.

The use of paper will prevent the hair from tangling with the rubber band and also prevent breakage. A length of ribbon or yarn may be attached to the topknot to dress up your Maltese.

If double topknots are desired, they are done in the same way, except that the hair is parted down the middle. Fold each topknot toward the side of the head.

BATHING THE MALTESE

If your Maltese is groomed regularly, he will need a bath only about once a month. Of course, if you are showing him at matches or kennel club shows, he will need to be bathed before each show.

Use a good quality shampoo designed for white coats, along with a conditioner prepared for the long-haired breeds. You will want to have a hair dryer, either a professional model or a simple hand-held type, to blow-dry the coat.

A laundry tub is ideal for bathing a Maltese, although there are any number of other possibilities including your kitchen sink. Just be certain to put a non-slip rubber mat at the bottom. Use warm water, shampoo twice, and then rinse thoroughly. Apply the conditioner and rinse again.

Remove your Maltese from the water, wrap him in a few bath towels, and begin drying him thoroughly. This may be a good time to clip his nails, as the toes show up better while the hair is still wet. Using clippers, trim the nails back almost to the pink or "quick" area. Continue the drying process with the assistance of a hair dryer, brushing your Maltese with a metal pin brush in the direction the hair is being blown. Do not let your Maltese run free until he is completely dry.

THE FINISHING TOUCHES

After your Maltese is completely dry, comb through his hair and prepare to attend to his feet and ears. Hair on the bottoms of the feet should be scissored off and the hair growing down inside the ears should be plucked out (carefully) with tweezers.

Put in the single or double topknot and then, with the comb, make a straight part down his back from just behind the topknot(s) to the base of the tail. Comb all the hair down, from the part, and you will see a happy, beautiful, well-groomed Maltese.

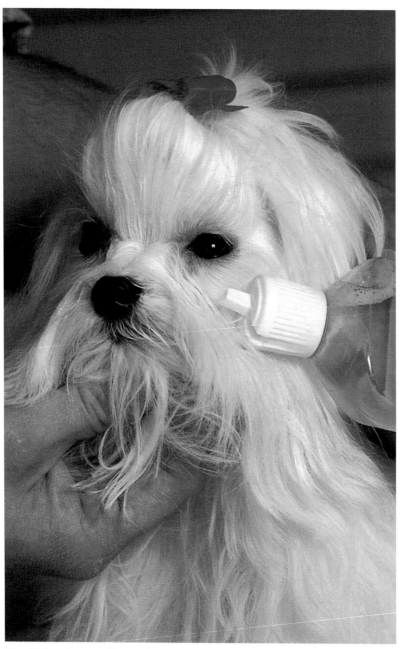

Many Maltese have problems with tearstains on their faces. Special eyewashes can be used to prevent eye irritation and remove the staining.

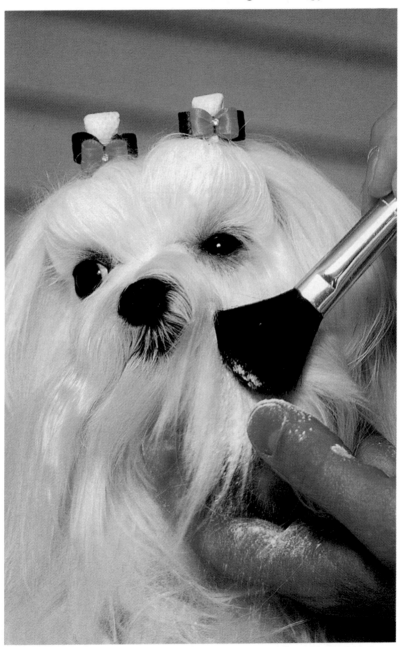

An alternative to using an eyewash to control tearstaining is boric acid powder. Brush or pat the powder onto the tearstained areas several times a day until they disappear.

SHORT AND SEMI-SHORT COATS

Many Maltese owners prefer to keep the coat cut short or semi-short. It depends entirely upon your own preference. It is obviously much easier to maintain a shorter coat. Your Maltese will still need to be brushed and combed, but not as often.

The shorter coat allows your dog to romp in leaves or snow. However, it also allows him to get wet and muddy, so care must be taken to make sure he is dry and clean whenever you bring him back inside.

If you choose to keep your Maltese in a shorter coat, even if only for a while, ask a professional groomer to clip the coat in a "puppy cut."

TEARSTAIN AND ITS CONTROL

Many Maltese have tearstain on their faces. This is the discoloration on the hair under the eyes, caused by excessive tearing of the eyes. Many other breeds of dog also have this, but it doesn't show up because their coats are not white like the Maltese coat. The staining in no way affects the health of your dog, but if you find the discoloration unattractive, there are ways of controlling it.

Some Maltese tear and stain more than others for various reasons. Likewise, there are times when an individual Maltese may stain more than other times. There are certain times of the year when the eyes may be more greatly affected by irritants such as pollen dust. A Maltese is likely to stain more while teething. Females sometimes stain when they are in season.

There are eyedrops that can be used for washing out dust and hair from the eyes. Put a few drops into the eyes and let the drops run down the stained hair. Boric acid powder can be brushed or patted on the wet, stained hair. Depending on how badly stained the hair is, you can apply the powder one to three times a day. Even after the staining is under control, you may prefer to wash your dog's eyes every day with either a commercial preparation or plain warm water. This will soothe his eyes, which accumulate dust and other irritants simply because he is so close to the ground.

To keep a clean white face, you may apply a little cornstarch just under the eyes and into the whiskers. The application can be made by using a toothbrush, although your own fingers will do just as well.

If your new puppy has stains on his face when you bring him home, you can start taking care of it right away. Most likely, the breeder did not want to put anything on the puppy's face because the dam and littermates habitually lick each other's faces.

NAIL CARE

Many dogs that run on gravel or pavement keep their toenails worn down, so they seldom need clipping. However, a dog that doesn't do much running or runs on grass will grow long toenails that can be harmful. Long nails will force the dog's toes into the air and spread his feet wide. In addition, the nails may force the dog into an unnatural stance that can produce lameness.

You can control your dog's toenails by cutting them with a special dog clipper or by filing them. Many dogs object to the clipping, and it takes some experience to learn just how to do it without cutting into the blood vessels (the quick). Your vet will probably examine your dog's nails whenever you bring him in and may trim them for you. He can show you how to do it yourself in the future. If you prefer, you can file the points off of your dog's nails every few weeks with a flat wooden file. Draw the file in only one direction—from the top of the nail downward, in a round stroke to the end of the nail or underneath. You'll need considerable pressure for the first few strokes to break through the hard surface, but then it gets easier. You may also use an electric nail grinder, but make sure you accustom the dog to the noise it makes first.

Incidentally, it's a good idea to keep your young puppy from walking on waxed or slippery floors, as this tends to break down the pasterns.

EAR CARE

Do not neglect your puppy's ears when going through your grooming steps, because it is very important to his health. Excessive dirt, moisture, and bacteria accumulating in the ear canal can cause ear infections. When taking care of your dog's ears, the first thing you should do is pluck or trim (with blunt-nosed scissors) the excess hair out. To keep them clean, use a cotton ball or washcloth dampened with commercial ear cleaner or mineral oil and wipe the inside of the earflap. If your puppy's ear is sore, has excess wax, or has a bad smell, he probably has an ear infection and needs to see the veterinarian immediately.

Never stick anything into your puppy's ear canal. When cleaning, wipe the outside area of the earflap only, or you may damage your dog's eardrum.

EYE CARE

It is fairly easy to keep your puppy's eyes clear, sparkling, and bright. First, make sure that you keep all debris (including hair) out

All dogs need to have their nails trimmed from time to time. Use a clipper or a grinder to trim the nail to an appropriate length.

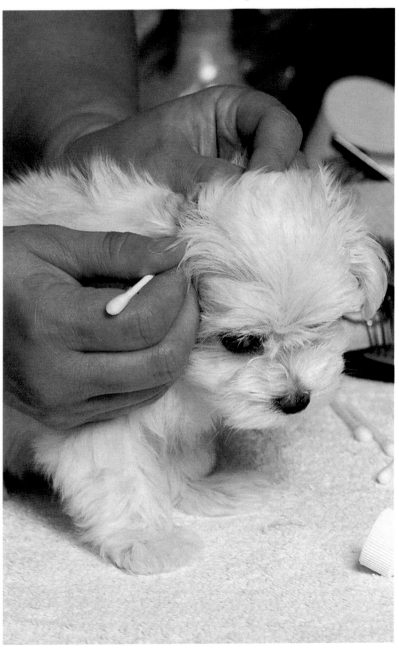

Your Maltese's ears need to be kept clean at all times. Wipe the ears with a soft, damp cloth or use a cotton swab to remove any dirt and wax buildup.

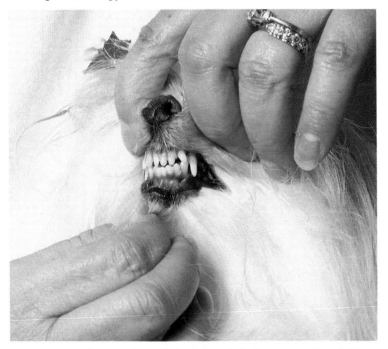

Your Maltese needs to have his teeth checked regularly. If you notice plaque build up, contact your veterinarian to have the teeth cleaned.

of his eyes. Wipe your dog's eyes on a regular basis with a cotton ball or washcloth dipped in warm water. If your puppy's eyes appear red, cloudy, or swollen, or have excess tearing, contact your veterinarian.

DENTAL CARE

Puppies need to chew. Chewing is an essential part of their physical and mental development, so you need to take good care of their teeth from the very beginning.

If you do not brush your dog's teeth on a regular basis, plaque builds up on the teeth and under the gums. If this plaque is not removed, periodontal disease, which is a bacterial infection, can occur. If left untreated, the bacteria can enter the bloodstream and spread to your puppy's vital organs. Other problems can develop as well, such as mouth abscesses and tooth loss. Also, puppies that don't receive good dental care can suffer from bad breath, a feature that does not endear them to humans or elicit doggy kisses.

The Maltese is a sturdy, strong little toy dog. With basic care, he will be your best friend.

It is much easier to brush your dog's teeth than you may think, as long as you have the right supplies. You should purchase a dog toothbrush or a finger toothbrush (a rubber cap that fits over your index finger) and toothpaste made for dogs. Start by accustoming your puppy to having your fingers in his mouth without brushing his teeth. When you are giving him his daily once-over, be sure to look in his mouth, exposing his gums and touching his teeth. Soon this will become just another part of his grooming routine.

Once he is used to this procedure, put some doggy-flavored toothpaste on the toothbrush and gently rub a few teeth at a time. Be sure to brush the teeth at the gum line. Use a circular motion when brushing and slowly make your way around your dog's upper teeth. Make sure to get the teeth in the back of the mouth, because these are the teeth most prone to periodontal disease. When you are finished with the top row, do the bottom row in the same manner.

Daily brushing would be ideal, but try to do it at least four times a week. This will ensure that your puppy keeps his teeth healthy and keeps them for a long time.

CHAPTER 4

Selecting Your Dog

Now that you have decided which breed of dog suits your needs, your lifestyle, and your temperament, there will be much to consider before you make your final purchase. Getting a puppy on impulse may only cause heartbreak later; it makes much more sense to put some real thought into your canine investment, especially because it is likely that he will share many happy years with you.

Once you've mulled over the pluses and minuses of dog ownership, ask yourself a few questions concerning your needs and preferences for a dog. Read all that you can about your particular breed,

Maltese puppies are absolutely adorable. Take your time and examine a number of pups before making your final selection.

When visiting a breeder, her Maltese should look healthy and loved. They should not shy away from people.

and visit a few dog shows. At the shows you will be surrounded by people who can give you all the details about the breed in which you are interested. Decide if you want a household pet or a show dog. Would you prefer a male or female? Puppy or adult?

If you buy from a breeder, ask to visit the premises and if possible, see the puppy's parents and other relatives. These breeders are always willing to discuss any breed problems and how they should be dealt with. This is also a good time to ask him to help you with your decision. When you have settled on the dog you want, discuss with the seller the dog's temperament, the animal's positive and negative aspects, any health problems he might have, his feeding and grooming requirements, and whether or not the dog has been immunized. Reputable sellers will be willing to answer any questions you might have that pertain to the dog you have selected, and often they will make themselves available if you call for advice or if you encounter problems after you've made your purchase.

Most breeders and sellers want to see their dogs placed in loving, responsible homes, so they are careful about who buys their animals.

Selecting the right Maltese should not be a quick decision. Remember that this dog will be living with you for many years to come.

Make sure you buy your Maltese pup from a reputable breeder. If you are not comfortable with a particular breeder or the way the puppies are handled or kept, visit another breeder.

Selecting Your Dog

As the dog's new owner, prepare yourself to answer some questions from the breeder.

WHERE TO BUY

You can choose among several places to buy your dog. One source is a kennel whose business is breeding show-quality dogs; such kennels may have extra pups for sale. Another source is the one-dog owner who wants to sell the puppies from an occasional litter to pay the expenses of his small-scale breeding operation. To find such kennels and part-time breeders and hobbyists, check the classified section of your local newspaper or look in your telephone directory. Whichever source you choose, you can usually tell in a very short time whether or not the puppies will make healthy and happy pets. If they are clean, plump, and lively, they are probably in good health. Sometimes you will have the advantage of seeing the puppies' dam and perhaps their sire and other relatives. Remember that the mother, having just raised a demanding family, may not be looking her best; but if she is sturdy, friendly, and well-mannered, her puppies should be too.

If you feel that something is lacking in the care or condition of the dogs, it is better to look elsewhere than to buy hastily and regret it afterward. Buy a healthy dog with a good disposition, one that has been properly socialized and likes being around people.

If you cannot find a local breeder, write to the secretary of the national breed club or kennel club and a reputable one will be recommended to you. Puppies are sometimes shipped to other states by reputable breeders. In these instances, pictures and pedigree information are usually sent beforehand to help you decide. Many breed clubs provide a puppy referral service, so you may want to look into this before making your final decision.

PET OR SHOW DOG

Conscientious breeders strive to maintain desirable qualities in their breeds. At the same time, they are always working to improve on what they have already achieved, and they do this by referring to the breed standard of perfection. The standard describes the ideal dog, and those animals that come close to the ideal are generally selected as show stock; those that do not are sold as pets. Keep in mind that pet-quality purebred dogs are in no way less healthy or attractive than show-quality specimens. Sometimes these dogs even prove more hardy. It's just that the pet may have features that would

Before you select a Maltese, you need to decide whether you want a pet- or show-quality dog.

be faults in the show ring. Often these so-called "flaws" are detectable only by experienced breeders or show judges.

If you are looking for a pet for the children or a companion for you, an older pup or a grown dog that is not being used for breeding or showing may be available.

The price you pay for your dog is little compared to the love and devotion he will return over the many years he'll be with you. With proper care and affection, your pup should live to a ripe old age; thanks to modern veterinary science and improvements in canine nutrition, dogs today are better maintained and live longer. It is not uncommon to see dogs living well into their teens.

ADULT OR PUP

Whether to buy a grown dog or a young puppy is an important decision. It is an undeniable pleasure to watch your dog grow from a lively pup to a mature, dignified dog. However, if you don't have the time to spend on frequent meals, housetraining, and other training that a puppy needs in order to become a dog you can be proud of, then choose an older, partly trained adolescent or a grown dog. If you want a show dog, remember that no one, not even an expert, can predict with 100-percent accuracy what a puppy will be like when

One particular Maltese pup may seem eager to become your pet. Ask to see this one away from his littermates to find out a bit more about his temperament and personality.

he grows up. Six months of age is the earliest age for the would-be exhibitor to select a prospect and know that his future is in the show ring. If you have a small child, it is best to get a puppy that is not less than four or five months old. Older children will enjoy playing with and helping to take care of a baby pup, but at less than four months of age, a puppy wants to do little else but eat and sleep. He must be protected from teasing and overexcitement. Children must learn how to handle and care for their young pets.

WHAT TO LOOK FOR IN A PUPPY

Make sure that the puppy you are considering comes from healthy, well-bred parents and is friendly and outgoing. If you want a show dog and have no experience in choosing a prospect, study the breed standard and listen carefully to the breeder about the finer points of show conformation. A breeder wants his top-quality show puppies placed in the public eye to reflect on his kennel and to attract future buyers.

Now that you have made your choice, you are ready to depart with puppy, papers, and instructions. Make sure that you know the youngster's feeding routine and take along some of his food. For the trip home, place him in a comfortable, sturdy carrier. Do not drive

Busy families and single adults don't always have the time to take care of a Maltese pup. Consider adopting an adult Maltese instead. Contact your local breed club or veterinarian for rescue organizations in your area.

A reputable breeder wants to see her pups go to loving, respectable homes and will ask you many questions to ensure the well-being of her Maltese.

home with a puppy on your lap! If you'll be traveling for a few hours, bring along a bottle of water from the breeder and a small water dish.

PEDIGREE AND REGISTRATION

The term "pedigree" is quite different from the term "registration." A pedigree is nothing more than a statement made by the breeder about the dog's lineage, and it will contain the names of several generations from which the new puppy comes. It records your puppy's ancestry and other important data, such as the pup's date of birth, his breed, his sex, his sire and dam, his breeder's name and address, and so on. If your dog has had purebred champions in his background, then the pedigree papers are valuable as evidence of the good breeding behind him; but if the names on the pedigree papers are meaningless, then so are the papers themselves. Just because a dog has a pedigree doesn't necessarily mean he is registered with a kennel club.

Registration papers from the American Kennel Club or the United Kennel Club in the United States or The Kennel Club of Great

The breeder should supply you with registration papers, a pedigree, a health record, and a diet sheet when you purchase your Maltese.

Britain attest to the fact that the mother and father of your puppy were purebred and that they were registered with a particular club. Normally, every registered dog also has a complete pedigree available. Registration papers, which you receive when you buy a puppy, enable you to register your puppy. Usually, the breeder has registered only the litter, so it is the new owner's responsibility to register and name an individual pup. The papers should be filled out and sent to the appropriate address printed on the application, along with the fee required for the registration. A certificate of registration will then be sent to you.

Pedigree and registration, by the way, have nothing to do with licensing, which is a local regulation. Find out what the local ordinance is in your town or city and how it applies to your dog, then buy a license and keep it on your dog's collar for identification.

CHAPTER 5

The New Family Member

At long last, the day you have all been waiting for will come, and your new puppy will make his grand entrance into your home. Before you bring your companion to his new residence, however, you must plan carefully for his arrival. Keep in mind that the puppy will need time to adjust to life with a different owner. He may seem a bit apprehensive about the strange surroundings in which he finds himself, having spent the first few weeks of life with his dam and littermates. In a couple of days, with love and patience on your part, the transition will be complete.

The puppy's first impressions are important, and these feelings may very well set the pattern of his future relationship with you. You must be consistent in the way you handle your pet so that he learns what is expected of him. He must come to trust and respect

Some advance preparation is needed before bringing your new Maltese home. Gates need to be placed to restrict the dog's movement in the home.

Pick up your new Maltese early in the day when you can spend lots of time with him. This will give him plenty of time to explore his new home with you there.

you as his keeper and master. When you provide him with proper care and attention, you will be rewarded with a loyal companion for many years. If you consider the needs of your puppy before you bring him home and plan accordingly, it will make the change from his former home to his new one easier.

ADVANCE PREPARATION

In preparing for your puppy's arrival, one of the most important things to find out from the seller is how the pup was maintained. What brand of food was offered, and when and how often was the puppy fed? Has the pup been housetrained; if so, what method was employed? At first, continue the routine started by the puppy's original owner; then, gradually, you can make changes that suit you and your lifestyle. If, for example, the puppy has been paper trained, plan to stock up on newspaper or specially made pads. Place these in a selected spot so that your puppy learns to use the designated area as his "bathroom." If you wish to train the puppy to eliminate outdoors, you can gradually move the area closer to the door, and eventually teach the puppy to go outside. Also, keep a supply of the dog food he has been eating on hand, because a sudden switch to new food could cause digestive upsets.

The New Family Member

Your Maltese needs a place to call his own. Have a comfortable bed ready for him when he arrives in your home.

Another consideration is sleeping and resting quarters. Be sure to supply a dog bed for your pup and introduce him to his special cozy corner so that he knows where to retire when he feels like taking a snooze. A crate is a great tool to use as your puppy's sleeping quarters, and also aids in the housetraining process. You'll need to buy a collar and leash, safe chew toys, and a few grooming tools as well. A couple of sturdy feeding dishes, one for food and one for water, will be also needed.

FINDING A VETERINARIAN

An important part of your preparations should include finding a local veterinarian who can provide quality health care in the form of routine checkups, inoculations, and prompt medical attention in case of illness or emergency. Find out if the puppy you have selected has been vaccinated against canine diseases and make certain you secure all health certificates at the time of purchase. This information will be valuable to your veterinarian, who will want to know the puppy's complete medical history. Don't wait until your puppy becomes sick before you seek the services of a vet; make an appointment for your pup before or soon after he takes up residence with you so that he starts out with a clean bill of health in his new home.

Children should be taught to treat a new Maltese gently and with care for both the dog's and the child's safety.

CHILDREN AND PUPPIES

If you have children at home, be sure to prepare them for the arrival of their new puppy. Children should learn not only to love their charges, but to respect them and treat them with the consideration that one would give all living things. It must be emphasized to youngsters that the puppy has certain needs, just as humans have,

Your new Maltese needs plenty of time outdoors to exercise. Supervise him at all times to keep him out of trouble.

and that all family members must take an active role in ensuring that these needs are met. Someone must feed the puppy, walk him a couple of times a day, groom his coat, clean his ears, and clip his nails. Someone must also see to it that the puppy gets sufficient exercise and attention each day.

A child who has a pet to care for learns responsibility; nonetheless, parental guidance is an essential part of this learning experience. You must teach your child how to carefully pick up and handle the pup. A dog should always be supported with both hands, not lifted by the scruff of the neck. One hand should be placed under the chest, between the front legs, and the other hand should support the dog's rear end.

BE A GOOD NEIGHBOR

For the sake of your dog's safety and well-being, don't allow him to wander onto the property of others. Keep him confined to your own yard at all times or on his leash when outside. There are many dangers for an unleashed dog, particularly when he is unsupervised by his master, including cars and trucks, stray animals, and poisonous substances. Also, dogs that are left to roam in a wooded area or

Lots of love and attention will make your new Maltese adjust to his new home faster.

field could become infected with any number of parasites. All these things can be avoided if you take precautions to keep your dog in a safe enclosure where he will be protected.

GETTING ACQUAINTED

If possible, plan to bring your new pet home in the morning so that by nightfall he will have had some time to become acquainted with you and his new environment. Avoid introducing the pup to the family around holiday time, because all of the extra excitement will only add to the confusion and frighten him. Let the puppy enter your home on a day when the routine is normal. For those people who work during the week, a Saturday morning is an ideal time to bring the puppy to his new home.

Let the puppy explore, under your watchful eye, of course, and let him investigate his new home without stress and fear. Resist the temptation to handle him too much during these first few days. If there are other dogs or animals around the house, make certain that all are properly introduced. If you observe fighting among the animals, you may have to separate all parties until they learn to accept

Socialization is very important for your new Maltese. After visiting your veterinarian and beginning the proper inoculations, gradually introduce your dog to other animals and people.

Adaptable to a variety of lifestyles, this energetic and pleasing dog is an ideal apartment dweller.

one another. Neglecting your other pets while showering the new puppy with extra attention will only cause animosity and jealousy. Make an effort to pay special attention to the other animals as well.

On that first night, your puppy may be frightened or lonely. It is all right to pay extra attention to him until he becomes used to his surroundings. Some people have had success with putting a doll or a hot water bottle wrapped in a towel in the puppy's bed as a surrogate mother, while others have placed a ticking alarm clock in the bed to simulate the heartbeat of the pup's dam and littermates. Remember that this furry little fellow is used to the warmth and security of his mother and siblings, so the adjustment to sleeping alone will take time. Select a sleeping location away from drafts and his feeding station. Keep in mind, also, that the bed should be roomy enough for him to stretch out in.

Prior to the pup's arrival, set up his room and partition it with gates or a pen to keep him in a safe enclosure. Wherever you decide to keep him, do it ahead of time so you will have that much less to worry about when your puppy finally moves in with you.

Once he becomes adjusted to living in your home, your Maltese will be a lifelong friend.

Give your new Maltese plenty of time to adjust. Patience, praise, and encouragement will help your pup feel welcomed into his new home.

Above all else, be patient with your puppy as he adjusts to life in his new home. If you purchase a pup that is not housetrained, you will have to spend lots of time with him—just as you would with a small child—until he develops proper toilet habits. Even a house-trained puppy may feel nervous in strange new surroundings and have an occasional accident. Praise and encouragement will elicit far better results than punishment or scolding. Remember that your puppy wants nothing more than to please you, and he is anxious to learn the behavior that is required of him.

CHAPTER 6

Feeding Requirements

Perhaps more than any other single aspect of your dog's development, proper feeding requires an educated and responsible dog owner. The importance of nutrition in relation to your dog's bone and muscle growth cannot be overemphasized.

Before you bring your puppy home, ask the seller what food was given and stay with that diet for awhile. If you prefer to switch to some other brand of dog food, begin to add small quantities of the

The number of feedings and the amount fed will vary as your Maltese gets older. Ask your veterinarian or breeder for help in setting up a feeding schedule.

Meals should be served at the same time every day. Your Maltese will get used to the schedule that you set.

new brand to the usual food offering. Make the portions of the new food progressively larger until the pup is weaned from his former diet. This will help to prevent stomach upsets.

What should you feed the puppy and how often? Puppies need to be fed small portions at frequent intervals, because they are growing and their activity level is high. You must ensure that your pup gains weight steadily. As your dog matures, his meals can be made larger and he can be fed once or twice a day, depending on his activity level. As far as the brand of dog food you choose is concerned, a great deal of money and research has resulted in foods that we can serve our dogs with confidence and pride, and most of these commercial foods have been developed along strict guidelines according to the size, weight, and age of your dog. These products are reasonably priced, easy to find, and convenient to store. Just be sure to read the label carefully to determine if the food is right for your dog's age, activity level, and development.

THE PUPPY'S MEALS

After a puppy has been fully weaned from his mother and until approximately three months of age, he needs to be fed four times a

Avoid feeding your Maltese immediately before or after he exercises. Digestive problems may result.

day. Offer him small meals that have been softened with water or milk. At six months of age, two meals are sufficient; at one year, a single meal can be given, supplemented with a few dry biscuits in the morning and evening. Always keep a bowl of cool, fresh water on hand to help your dog regulate his body temperature and to aid in digestion.

From one year of age on, you may continue feeding the mature dog a single meal or you may prefer to divide this meal in two, offering half in the morning and the other half at night. Discuss your dog's feeding schedule with your veterinarian; he can make suggestions about the right diet for your particular canine friend.

FACTORS AFFECTING NUTRITIONAL NEEDS

Activity Level. A dog that lives in a country environment and is able to exercise for long periods of the day will need more food than the same breed of dog living in an apartment and given little exercise. Likewise, a working country canine would burn up more calories than one that simply lived in the country and received plenty of exercise.

There are many different types of pet food in the stores today. Try to continue using the brand that was given to your Maltese by the breeder.

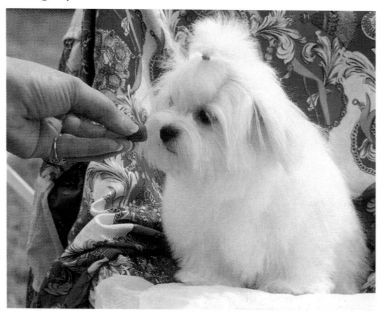

Give your Maltese treats throughout the day, but remember that these treats should be nutritious and are a part of his daily food intake.

Quality of the Food. Obviously, the quality of food will affect the quantity required by a puppy. If the nutritional content of a food is low, then the puppy will need more of it than a better quality food.

Balance of Nutrients and Vitamins. Feeding a puppy the correct balance of nutrients is not easy, because the average person is not able to measure out ratios of one to another, so it is a case of trying to see that nothing is in excess. However, only tests or your veterinarian can be the source of reliable advice.

Genetic and Biological Variation. Apart from all of the other considerations, it should be remembered that each puppy is an individual. His genetic makeup will influence not only his physical characteristics, but also his metabolic efficiency. This being so, two pups from the same litter can vary quite a bit in the amount of food they need to perform the same function under the same conditions. If you consider the potential combinations of all of these factors, you will see that pups of a given breed could vary quite a bit in the amount of food they will need. Before discussing feeding quantities, it is valuable to know at least a little about the composition of food and its role in the body.

Your Maltese pup will need to eliminate almost immediately after eating. Take your pup to a potty area when he finishes his meal and praise him when he eliminates.

COMPOSITION AND ROLE OF FOOD

The main ingredients of food are protein, fats, and carbohydrates, each of which is needed in relatively large quantities when compared to the need for vitamins and minerals. The other vital ingredient of food is, of course, water. Although all foods obviously contain some of the basic ingredients needed for an animal to survive, they do not all contain the ingredients in the needed ratios or types. For example, there are many forms of protein, just as there are many types of carbohydrates. Both of these compounds are found in meat and in vegetable matter—but not all of those that are needed will be in one particular meat or vegetable. Plants, especially, do not contain certain amino acids that are required for the synthesis of certain proteins needed by dogs.

Likewise, vitamins are found in meat and vegetable matter, but vegetables are a richer source of most. Meat contains very little carbohydrates. Some vitamins can be synthesized by the dog, so they do

Fresh, clean water is as important to your Maltese's health as nutritious food. Make sure he has plenty of water, especially on hot days.

not need to be supplied via the food. Dogs are omnivores, which means that they digest both meat and vegetable matter.

In order to gain its needed vegetable matter in a form that it can cope with, the carnivore eats all of its prey. This includes the partly digested food within the stomach. In commercially prepared foods, the cellulose is broken down by cooking. During this process, the vitamin content is either greatly reduced or lost altogether. The manufacturer, therefore, adds vitamins once the heat process, has been completed. This is why commercial foods are so useful as part of a feeding regimen, providing they are of good quality and from a company that has prepared the foods very carefully.

Proteins: These are made from amino acids, of which at least ten are essential if a puppy is to maintain healthy growth. Proteins provide the building blocks for the puppy's body. The richest sources are meat, fish, and poultry, together with their by-products. The latter will include milk, cheese, yogurt, fishmeal, and eggs. Vegetable matter that has a high protein content includes soy beans, together with numerous corn and other plant extracts that have been dehydrated. The actual protein content needed in the diet will be determined both by the activity level of the dog and his age. The total protein need will also be influenced by the digestibility factor of the food given.

Fats: These serve numerous roles in the puppy's body. They provide insulation against the cold and help buffer the organs from knocks and general activity shocks. They provide the richest source of energy, and reserves of it, and they are vital in the transport of vitamins and other nutrients, via the blood, to all other organs. Finally, it is the fat content within a diet that gives it palatability, although it is important that it not be excessive. This is because the high energy content of fats (more than twice that of proteins or carbohydrates) will increase the overall energy content of the diet. The puppy will adjust his food intake to that of his energy needs, which are obviously more easily met in a high-energy diet. This will mean that while fats are providing the energy needs of the puppy, the overall diet may not be providing his protein, vitamin, and mineral needs, so signs of protein deficiency will become apparent. Rich sources of fats are those of meat, their by-products (butter, milk), and vegetable oils, such as safflower, olive, corn, or soy bean.

Carbohydrates: These are the principle energy compounds given to puppies and adult dogs. Their inclusion within most commercial brand dog foods is for cost, rather than dietary needs. These compounds are more commonly known as sugars, and they

Feed your Maltese the type of food that is formulated for his stage of development and his special needs. If you are unsure as to which food to choose, consult your veterinarian or breeder for recommendations.

are seen in simple or complex compounds of carbon, hydrogen, and oxygen. One of the simple sugars is called glucose, and it is vital to many metabolic processes. When large chains of glucose are created they form compound sugars. One of these is called glycogen, and it is found in the cells of animals. Another, called starch, is the material that is found in the cells of plants.

Vitamins: These are not foods as such but chemical compounds that assist in all aspects of an animal's life. They help in so many ways that to attempt to describe them effectively would require a chapter in itself. Fruits are a rich source of vitamins, as are the livers of most animals. Many vitamins are unstable and easily destroyed by light, heat, moisture, or rancidity. An excess of vitamins, especially A and D, has been proven to be very harmful. Provided a puppy is receiving a balanced diet, it is most unlikely there will be a deficiency, whereas hypervitaminosis (an excess of vitamins) has become quite common due to owners and breeders feeding unneeded supplements. The only time you should feed extra vitamins to your puppy is if your veterinarian advises you to do so.

Minerals: These provide strength to bone and cell tissue, as well as assisting in many metabolic processes. Examples are calcium, phosphorous, copper, iron, magnesium, selenium, potassium, zinc, and sodium. The full dietary need for all minerals has not been fully established. Calcium and phosphorous are known to be important, especially to puppies. They help in forming strong bone. As with vitamins, a mineral deficiency is most unlikely in pups given a good and varied diet. Again, an excess can create problems—this applying particularly to calcium.

Water: This is the most important of all nutrients, as is easily shown by the fact that the adult dog is made up of about 60 percent water, the puppy containing an even higher percentage. Dogs must retain a water balance, which means that the total intake should be balanced by the total output. The intake comes either by direct input (the tap or its equivalent), plus water released when food is oxidized, known as metabolic water (all foods contain the elements hydrogen and oxygen, which recombine in the body to create water). A dog without adequate water will lose condition more rapidly than one depleted of food, a fact common to most animal species.

READING LABELS

There are two agencies that work together in regulating pet food labels. The first agency, the Association of American Feed Control

Your Maltese should have manners when it is mealtime. Have your dog assume the sit position until the food is placed on the floor.

Officials (AAFCO), is a nongovernmental agency made up of state and federal officials from around the United States. They establish pet food regulations that are more specific and cover areas like guaranteed analysis, nutritional adequacy statements, and feeding directions. Each states decides whether or not to enforce AAFCO's regulations—most do; however, some do not.

The second agency, the Food and Drug Administration Center for Veterinary Medicine, establishes and enforces standards for all animal feed. This federal agency oversees aspects of labeling that cover proper identification of product, net quantity statements, and the list of ingredients.

Learning how to read the labels of dog food is important, especially when you consider how many brands are out there. Slight changes in wording can make the difference between a quality dog food and one that may not appear to be what it seems.

PRODUCT NAME

You may think the name of your dog food is just the name—but in this case, it can make a big difference. Specific words used in the

Given the proper diet of a nutritious dog food with a growth formula, your Maltese pup will grow to be a happy, healthy adult.

name can indicate what is in the food and what is not. For example, a brand name like "Beef Dog Food" must contain at least 95 percent beef, but if it is called "Beef *Formula* for Dogs," it is required to contain a minimum of only 25 percent beef. Other words like dinner, platter, nuggets, or entrée fall under this 25 percent minimum requirement.

Another word to watch for is "with." A dog food called "Dog Food with Beef" only has to contain a minimum of three percent beef. The word "with" was originally supposed to highlight extra ingredients, but recent amendments to AAFCO regulations now allow the word to be used in the product's name. Also, the word "flavored" can be deceiving, because it means that only a sufficient amount of flavoring needs to be added for it to be detectable. Therefore, "Beef Flavored Dog Food" may not include any beef at all and may only be flavored with very small amounts of beef by-products.

INGREDIENT LIST

Each ingredient contained in the dog food will be listed in descending order according to weight, but the quality of the ingredient is not required to be listed. For best results, look for animal-based proteins to be high up on the list, such as beef, beef by-products, chicken, chicken by-products, lamb, lamb meal, fish meal, and egg. However, use caution and read carefully, because some manufacturers will manipulate the weight of products in order to place them higher or lower on the list. For example, they may divide the grains into different categories, like wheat flour and whole ground wheat, in order to lower the weight and make them seem less prominent on the ingredient list.

What exactly are meat by-products and meal, anyway? Actual "meat" is considered to be the clean flesh of a slaughtered mammal and is limited to the part of the striate muscle that is skeletal or found in the tongue, diaphragm, heart, or esophagus. Meat by-products are the nonrendered lean parts other than the meat, which includes, but is not limited to, the lungs, spleen, kidney, bone, blood, stomach, intestines, necks, feet, and undeveloped eggs. Meat and bone meal are the rendered product or mammal tissue, which includes bone, hair hood, horn, hide trimming, manure, and stomach. As you can see, the ingredients in dog food can vary widely, which is why it is so important to be informed about what your puppy is actually eating.

GUARANTEED ANALYSIS

The guaranteed analysis states the minimum amount of crude protein and crude fat, as well as the maximum amount percentage of moisture (water) and crude fiber. The word "crude" refers to the method of testing the product, not the quality of the nutrient. Sometimes manufactures will list other nutrients like ash or calcium, although they are not required to do so.

NUTRITIONAL ADEQUACY STATEMENT

The nutritional adequacy statement is important when looking for a dog food for puppies, because it states what life stage the product is formulated for, such as growth, reproduction, maintenance, senior, or all life stages. For best results for developing puppies, look for the product that is especially formulated for growth. It should also tell you whether the product is "complete and balanced" or "complementary." Complete and balanced means that it contains all the ingredients that your dog will need on a daily basis and that it can serve by itself as a meal. Complementary means that it is not intended to be used as a meal and must be added to another product to create one.

NET QUANTITY STATEMENT

The net quantity statement shows the weight of the food in the bag or can in pounds and ounces and in metric weight. Be careful, because some companies use 30-pound bags and then only put 25 pounds of food inside.

FEEDING INSTRUCTIONS

The feeding instructions on the dog food label are only suggestions; some dogs will eat more, some will eat less. Also, they are the amounts needed for the entire day, so you can break it up the best way for you and your puppy by dividing how many meals you feed a day by the total amount. If you are not sure how much to feed, start off with the suggested amount and increase or decrease as necessary.

Although dog food labels tell you a lot about a product, there is a lot they don't tell you. For example, some wording used on labels can be misleading. Foods that use the words "gourmet" or "premium" are not required to contain any higher quality ingredients than any other product. Products that claim to be "all-natural" are not required to be so. Some might think that this means that the food is

As your Maltese matures, he may require a special diet. Discuss any dietary changes with your veterinarian and make them gradually.

minimally processed or contains no artificial ingredients, but this is not necessarily true. In fact, all dog foods must contain some chemically synthesized ingredients in order to be deemed complete and balanced.

HOMEMADE DIETS

There seems to be a debate about whether a homemade diet is better for your dog than a manufactured dog food. The downside to feeding a homemade diet is that you need to be very careful in order to ensure that you are providing your puppy with all of the nutrients he requires. It also takes a lot of time, effort, and energy to cook a proper diet for your dog on a daily basis.

MALTESE

Those that are in favor of a homemade diet believe that commercial dog foods contain contaminated and unhealthy ingredients and feel that it is worth the effort to give their puppy a homecooked meal.

If you have the time, the money, and the belief that it is important to feed your puppy a homemade diet, make sure you consult your veterinarian who can give you a reputable and nutritionally balanced recipe. Although millions of dogs exist and stay healthy on commercially prepared dog food, the ultimate decision is yours to make.

FEEDING GUIDELINES

• Nutritional balance, provided by many commercial dog foods, is vital; avoid feeding a one-sided all-meat diet. Variety in the kinds of meat (beef, lamb, chicken, liver) or cereal grains (wheat, oats, corn) that you offer your dog is of secondary importance compared to the balance or "completeness" of dietary components.

• Always refrigerate opened canned food so that it doesn't spoil. Remember to remove all uneaten portions of canned or moistened food from the feeding dish as soon as the pup has finished his meal. Discard the leftover food immediately and thoroughly wash and dry the feeding dish, as a dirty dish is a breeding ground for harmful germs.

• Always keep a supply of water on hand for your dog. Each day the water dish should be washed with soap and hot water, rinsed well, and dried; a refill of clean, fresh water should be provided daily.

• Food and water should be served at room temperature, neither too hot nor too cold, so that it is more palatable for your puppy.

• Serve your pup's meals in sturdy hard-plastic, stainless steel, or earthenware containers, ones that won't tip over as the dog gulps his food down. Some bowls and dishes are weighted to prevent spillage, while others fit neatly into holders that offer support. Feeding dishes should be large enough to hold each meal.

• As your dog matures, he may need a special diet. Dogs with health problems, such as obesity, pregnant and nursing mothers, and senior dogs all have special dietary needs. Always contact your vet for advice on these requirements.

• Reserve treats for special occasions or to reward good behavior during training sessions. Always make them nutritious.

• Hard foods, such as biscuits and dog meal, should be offered regularly. Chewing on these hard, dry morsels helps the dog keep his teeth clean and his gums conditioned.

• Do not encourage your dog to beg for food from the table while you are eating your meals.

CHAPTER 7

Accommodations

Puppies newly weaned from their mothers and separated from their siblings should be kept warm at all times. As they get older, they can be acclimated gradually to cooler temperatures. Although some breeds adapt better to the outdoors than others, all dogs deserve to be allowed to live inside with their families. They also are

Unless you plan to share your favorite chair with your dog all the time, your Maltese should be trained to stay off of it.

Give your Maltese a place to call his own. His bed should be placed in a warm, dry, draft-free area.

entitled to a safe outside environment with shelter from the elements. For the time that your dog will spend indoors, a dog bed in the corner of the family room will suffice, or you may want to invest in a crate for him to "call his home" whenever he needs to be confined for short intervals. You might plan to partition off a special room or part of a room for your pooch, or you may find that a heated garage or finished basement works well as your dog's living quarters. For the time that your dog will spend outside, you may want to buy or build him his own dog house with an attached run or place his house in your fenced-in backyard. All dogs need access to some sort of warm, dry shelter during periods of inclement weather. As you begin thinking about where your canine friend will spend most of his time, you'll want to consider his coat type, his age, his temperament, his need for exercise, and the money, space, and resources you have available to house him.

THE DOG BED

In preparing for your puppy's arrival, it is recommended that a dog bed be waiting for him so that he has a place to sleep and rest. If you

Changing the pup's bedding if it is soiled or dirty will help to keep him in good health.

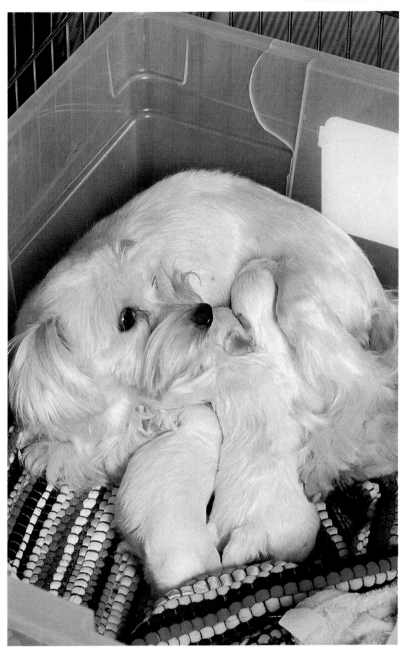

Providing a blanket for your dog will help keep him warm on those cold winter nights.

Your Maltese needs toys to keep him busy. A few toys, such as those made by Nylabone®, in his bed may help to keep him from feeling lonely at night.

have provided him with his own bed or basket, make sure that it is placed in a warm, dry, draft-free spot that is private but at the same time near the center of family activity. Refrain from placing his bed near his food and water dishes. You may want to give your puppy something to snuggle, such as a laundered towel or blanket or an article of old clothing. Some dogs have been known to chew apart their beds and bedding, but you can easily channel this chewing energy into more constructive behavior by simply supplying him with some safe toys to chew on. Pet shops stock dog beds, among other supplies that you might need for your pup. Select a bed that is roomy, comfortable, and easy to clean, keeping in mind that you may have to replace the smaller bed with a larger one as the puppy grows to adulthood. Remember to clean and disinfect the bed and sleeping area regularly.

THE CRATE

Many people cringe at the word crate because they think of it as a cage or a cruel means of confinement. However, this handy piece of equipment can be put to good use for puppies and grown dogs alike. Even though you love your dog, you may not want him to have free reign of the house, particularly when you are not home to supervise him. If used properly, a crate can restrict your dog when it is not convenient to have him underfoot—keeping both the dog and your belongings safe.

A surprising number of dog owners who originally had negative feelings about crating their dogs have had great success using crates. The crate can serve as a bed, provided it is furnished with bedding material, or it can be used as an indoor dog house. You can use it to confine your dog for a few hours while you are away from home or at work, or you can bring your crated dog along with you in the car when you travel or go on vacation. Crates also prove handy whenever you have to transport a sick dog to the veterinarian.

Most crates are made of sturdy wire or plastic, and those made by Nylabone® can be conveniently stored or folded so that they can be moved easily. You can allow your puppy or grown dog to become acquainted with his crate by propping the door open and leaving some of his favorite toys inside. He will come to regard it as his own doggie haven in no time. As with a dog bed, place the crate away from drafts in a dry, warm spot and refrain from placing food and water dishes in it, as these only crowd the space and offer opportunity for spillage.

When choosing a crate for your dog, select one in which the dog can stand up and move around comfortably. Never leave the dog confined in his crate for more than a few hours at a time without letting him out to exercise, play, and, if necessary, relieve himself.

Crates can also be a useful tool when housetraining. Because dogs do not like to soil where they eat or sleep, your puppy will wait until you take him outside to relieve himself. By confining him in his crate, you are reducing the chances that he will have an accident in the house.

THE DOG HOUSE

These structures, often made of wood, should be sturdy and offer enough room for your dog to stretch out in when he rests or sleeps. Dog houses that are elevated or situated on a platform protect the animal from cold and dampness that may seep through the ground. For the breeds that are hardy and enjoy the outdoors, a dog house in a secure, fenced-in area is an excellent place to keep them if you are not at home during the day.

Some fortunate owners whose yards are enclosed by high fences can allow their dogs complete freedom within the boundaries of their

Maltese love to be outdoors. If possible, provide your dog with a dog run or a dog house of his own in your yard.

property. In these situations, a dog can leave his dog house and get all the exercise he wants. Of course, such a large space requires more effort to keep clean. An alternative to complete backyard freedom is a dog kennel or run that attaches to or surrounds the dog's house. These runs provide ample room for walking, climbing, jumping, and stretching. Another option is to fence off part of the yard and place the dog house in the enclosure.

CLEANLINESS

No matter where your dog lives, either in or out of your home, be sure to keep him in surroundings that are as clean and sanitary as possible. You should clean up after your dog every day. If your dog lives in his own house, the floor should be swept occasionally and the bedding should be changed regularly. Food and water dishes need to be scrubbed with hot water and detergent and rinsed well to remove all traces of soap. The water dish should be refilled with a constant supply of fresh water. The dog and his environment must be kept free of parasites (especially fleas and mosquitoes, which can carry disease) with products designed to keep these pests under control. Dog crates need frequent scrubbing, too, as do the

MALTESE   **87**

Young Maltese pups, like all puppies, have no control over their bowels or bladders. Spreading newspaper around the bed will help make the cleanup of accidents easier.

floors of kennels and runs. Your pet must be kept clean and comfortable at all times; if you exercise strict sanitary control, you will keep disease and parasite infestation to a minimum.

EXERCISE

A well-balanced diet and regular medical attention from a qualified veterinarian are essential in promoting your dog's good health, but so is daily exercise. This keeps him fit and mentally alert. Dogs that have been confined all day while their owners are at work or school need special attention. There should be some time set aside each day for play, as well as walks after each meal so that they can relieve themselves.

Whenever possible, take a stroll to an empty lot, a playground, or a nearby park. Attach a long lead to your dog's collar. This will help him burn calories, keep trim, and relieve tension and stress that may have had a chance to develop while you were away all day. For people who work during the week, weekend jaunts can be especially beneficial, because you have more time to spend with your canine

Accommodations

Regular exercise is important to maintaining your Maltese's health. If you are leaving him outside while away, make sure he has plenty of toys to keep him occupied. Also provide him with plenty of food and water, as well as shelter to keep him safe from the elements.

If you cannot supervise your Maltese, he should be in a fenced-in area to help keep him safe.

friend. Games and fun are very important, too, not only for your dog's well-being, but also as a means of creating a strong bond between dogs and owners. You might want to engage your dog in a simple game of fetch with a stick or a rubber ball. Teaching him basic tricks such as rolling over, standing on his hindlegs, or jumping up (all of which can be done inside the home as well) can provide additional exercise. If you plan to challenge your dog with a real workout, remember not to push him too hard without first warming up with a brisk walk. Don't forget to "cool him down" afterward with a rhythmic trot until his heart rate returns to normal. Some dog owners jog with their dogs or take them along on bicycle excursions. Never push your dog too hard; regular extensive training should only be done with adult dogs, never puppies. You should also work up to maximum speed very slowly, working in short time intervals at first, then building up the length of the workouts as your dog improves his condition.

At the very least, however, play with your dog every day to keep him in good shape, physically and mentally. If you can walk him outdoors or better yet run with him in a more vigorous activity, by all means do it. Don't neglect your pet and leave him confined for long periods without giving him attention or time for exercise.

CHAPTER 8

Housetraining and Basic Training

The new addition to your family may already have received some basic housetraining before his arrival in your home. A puppy will want to relieve himself about half a dozen times a day; it is up to you to specify where and when he should do it. Housetraining is your first training concern and should begin the moment you bring the puppy home.

Ideally, a puppy should be taken outdoors to eliminate. The best times to take him outside are first thing in the morning, after each meal, after naps, after play times, and before bedtime at night. When he eliminates, he should be praised. He should also be encouraged to use the same area and will probably be attracted to it after frequent use.

You should use the same command when you take your puppy outside so that your pet will associate the act of elimination with a particular

Potty training will be much easier for your Maltese pup if you continually bring him back to the same spot to eliminate.

word of your choice. Some words to use are "go," "hurry," "potty," or anything else you feel comfortable saying. The shorter the word, the more you can repeat it and imprint it on your dog's memory.

It is important to familiarize yourself with the telltale signs preceding your puppy's elimination process. There is usually a sense of urgency on the dog's part; he may follow a sniffing and circling pattern, which you will soon recognize. Remember that any training takes time. Such a conditioned response can be obtained with intensive practice with any normal, healthy dog over six weeks of age. Patience and persistence will eventually produce results.

Although it is not ideal, some people may prefer to allow their dogs to eliminate in a designated spot inside. In this case, sheets of newspaper or special pads can be used to cover the specific area where your dog should relieve himself. These should be placed some distance away from his sleeping and feeding area, because a puppy will not urinate or defecate where he eats. When the papers or pads are changed, the bottom one should be placed on top of the new ones in order to reinforce the scent. The puppy should be praised during or immediately after he has made use of this particular part of the room. Each positive reinforcement increases the possibility of his using that area again.

When your puppy arrives, it is advisable to limit him to one room, usually the kitchen, as it most likely has a linoleum or easily washable floor surface. If he is given the run of the house, it will be overwhelming and confusing and he might leave his "signature" on your furniture or clothes. There will be time later to familiarize him gradually with his new surroundings.

PATIENCE, PERSISTENCE, AND PRAISE

As with a human baby, you must be patient, tolerant, and understanding of your pet's mistakes, making sure he feels loved and wanted. A young puppy does not have full control of his body functions and does not eliminate on purpose. Never punish the pup for having an accident in the house, especially if you do not catch him in the act. Yelling, hitting, or rubbing his nose in it will teach him only to fear you. If you happen to catch your puppy in the act of eliminating indoors, firmly tell him, "No," and take him outside. If you are diligent about getting him outside often enough, he will soon learn what is expected of him.

Most puppies are eager to please. Praise, encouragement, and reward (particularly the food variety) will produce far better results than any scolding or physical punishment.

Familiarize yourself with the telltale signs that your pup needs to be taken outside to eliminate.

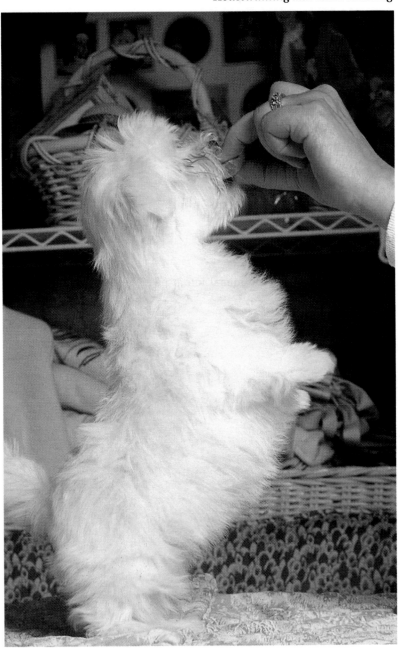

Praise and reward your Maltese for successfully completing a command. The positive reinforcement and the treat will make him want to continue to please you.

Housetraining and Basic Training

Usually, the reason a dog has housetraining or behavior problems is because his owner has allowed them to develop. This is why you must let your dog know what is acceptable and unacceptable behavior from the very beginning. It is also important that you are consistent in your demands; you cannot feed him from the dining room table one day and then punish him when he begs for food from your dinner guests.

TRAINING

You will want the newest member of your family to be a polite dog that is welcomed by everyone. In order to accomplish this, he needs training in the correct forms of behavior. You cannot expect your puppy to become the perfect pet overnight. He needs your help in his socialization process. Training greatly facilitates and enhances the relationship of the dog to his owner and to the rest of society. A successfully trained dog can be taken anywhere and behave well with anyone. Indeed, it is that one crucial word—training—that can transform an aggressive animal into a peaceful, well-behaved pet. Now, how does this "transformation" take place?

Every dog has the right to be trained. Teach your Maltese exactly which behaviors are tolerated and which ones are not.

Before going out, make sure your dog is wearing his leash. Never allow your Maltese to roam or run loose when out in public.

WHEN AND HOW TO TRAIN

Like housetraining, training should begin as soon as the puppy enters the house. The formal training sessions should be short but frequent, for example, 10 to 15 minute periods 3 times a day. You are building your relationship with your puppy during these times, so make them as enjoyable as possible. Pick times of the day when your puppy is alert and active. Just before his meals is ideal because he will be more motivated, especially if you reward him with treats.

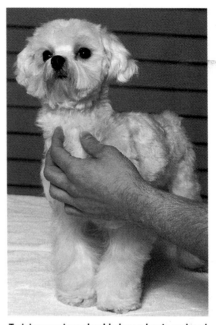

Training sessions should always begin and end on a positive note.

THE COLLAR AND LEASH

Your puppy should become used to a collar and leash as soon as possible. Have his name and address on an identification tag attached to his collar, as you don't want to lose your pet if he should happen to leave your premises and explore the neighborhood.

Let the puppy wear his collar until he is used to how it feels. After a short time, he will soon become accustomed to it, and you can attach the leash. He might resist your attempts to lead him or simply sit down and refuse to budge. Allow him to wander around with the leash until he begins to get used to the feel of it. Keep in mind that a dog's period of concentration is short, so make training sessions brief and always end on a high note, with play and praise. Most of all, remember that patience is the password to success.

GIVING COMMANDS

When you begin giving your puppy simple commands, make them as short as possible and use the same word with the same meaning at all times. You must be consistent or your puppy will become confused. Do not become impatient with him however many times you have to repeat your command.

MALTESE

COME

One of the most important commands your puppy will learn is to come when called. This is important for his safety. The best way to teach this command is to keep your dog on a long leash. Let him wander and explore for a while, then call him to you. If he comes right away, give him a treat and lots of praise. If he doesn't, do not repeat the command. Just pull him toward you with the leash. When he gets to you, praise him anyway so that he associates coming to you with positive results. A good way to introduce the come command is to call the puppy when his meal is ready. Once this is learned, you can call your pet to you at will, always remembering to praise him for his

Your Maltese must be taught that commands must be followed. Never give a command that you are not willing to enforce.

prompt obedience. This "reward," or positive reinforcement, is a crucial part of training. If you use the command, "Come," use it every time. Don't switch to "Come here" or "Come boy," as this will only confuse your dog.

Never punish your dog if he does not come when called. This will teach him to associate coming to you with negative results. Just keep trying, and he will eventually learn that it's in his best interest to come when called.

SIT

The sit command is one of the easiest and most useful commands for your dog to learn, so it is a good idea to begin with it. The only equipment required is a leash, a collar, and a few tasty tidbits. Take your dog out for some exercise before his meal. Have a few nutritious

Training commands can begin almost as soon as you bring your new Maltese home. If you allow your dog to get away with misbehavior as a pup, he will not obey as an adult.

Never scold or yell at your Maltese for not following a command. Simply put him in the last correct position and continue from there.

treats that your dog likes with you. After about five minutes, call him to you, and praise him when he arrives. Tell him, "Sit," in a loud, clear voice. As you say the command, take a treat and raise it from in front of his nose to directly over his head. As he follows the treat, he should automatically go into the sit position. Praise him and give him the treat for a job well done. If your dog still won't sit after a few tries, tell him, "Sit," and gently press on his rump until he is in a sitting position. As soon as he is in the correct position, praise him and give him the tidbit you have in your hand. Now wait a few minutes to let him rest and repeat the routine. Through repetition, the dog will soon associate the word with the act. Never make the lesson too long. Eventually, your praise will be reward enough for your puppy.

SIT-STAY/STAY

To teach your pet to remain in one place or "stay" on your command, first order him to sit at your side. Lower your left hand with the flat of your palm in front of his nose and your fingers pointing downward. Say, "Sit, stay," and, as you say it, step in front of him. If

One of the easiest commands to teach your Maltese is to sit. Most dogs will master it very quickly.

The down command is a difficult one for your dog to learn. The down position in the dog's pack is a sign of being submissive.

your dog stays in position, praise him and give him a treat. If he breaks the stay and comes to you, simply place him back in position and try again. This command is especially hard for young puppies, so remember to make the lessons short at first. You can gradually build up the time that your dog stays in position as he matures.

HEEL

When you walk your dog, you should hold the leash firmly in your right hand. The dog should walk on your left, so you have the leash crossing your body. This enables you to have greater control over the dog.

Let your dog lead you for the first few moments so that he fully understands that freedom can be his if he goes about it properly. He already knows that when he wants to go outdoors the leash and collar are necessary, therefore he has respect for the leash.

Once the puppy obeys the pull of the leash, half of your training is accomplished. Heeling is a necessity for a well-behaved dog, so teach him to walk beside you, head even with your knee.

To teach your dog this command, start off walking briskly, saying, "Heel," in a firm voice. Pull back with a sharp jerk if he lunges ahead, and if he lags, repeat the command and tug on the leash, not allowing him to drag behind. After the dog has learned to heel at various speeds on leash, you can remove it and practice heeling free, but have it ready to snap on again as soon as he wanders.

DOWN

Teaching the down command ideally begins while your dog is still a pup. During puppyhood, your dog will frequently lie down, as this is one of the dog's most natural positions. Keep close watch over your pup, and each time he begins to lie down, repeat the command, "Down," in a low convincing tone. Eventually, he should associate the motion with the command. Remember to praise him every time he lies down.

Teaching the down command to a mature dog will require more effort. Although the lying position is still natural to a dog, his being forced into it is not. Have your dog sit and face you. If he is responsive and congenial, gently take his paws, and slowly pull them

A Maltese pup will be easier to train than an adult dog. Consider this when making your selection.

toward you; give the down command as he approaches the proper position. Praise him for a job well done. Repeat several times: Moderate reinforcement of this procedure should prove rewardingly successful.

Daily reinforcement of the training method will soon yield the desired results. The keys to remember are: patience, persistence, and praise.

THE CANINE GOOD CITIZEN® TEST

As discussed before, all puppies should have the benefit of basic training. A good way to make sure that your puppy has the good manners he will need is to train for the Canine Good Citizen® Test. The American Kennel Club (AKC) has developed this program to encourage all owners to properly train their dogs. It emphasizes responsible dog ownership and teaching your puppy good manners in the home and in the community. All dogs of any age, purebred or mixed breed, can take the Canine Good Citizen® Test and earn a certificate from the AKC, as well as the right to add the title of CGC® to their names.

Training your Maltese for the Canine Good Citizen® Test will ensure that he has good manners and will be welcomed anywhere.

The sit command should be given to your Maltese at the beginning of each training session, because it is the foundation of all the other commands.

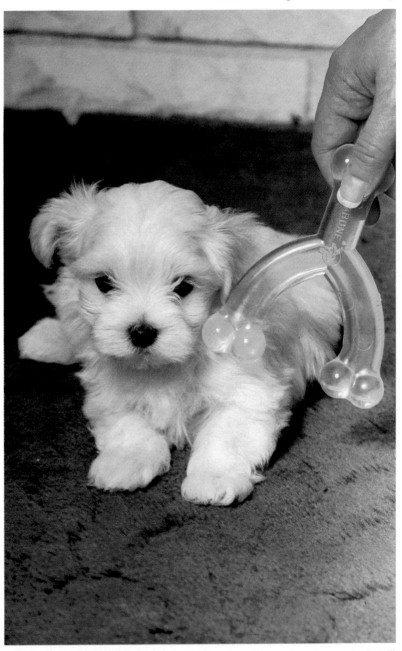

It's never too early to begin training your Maltese puppy. Good training ensures that he will become a well-mannered adult.

Housetraining and Basic Training

The dog must complete ten steps in order to pass. He must prove that he is a dog that any person would like to own, that he is safe with children, that he would be welcomed as a neighbor, and that he makes his owner happy while not making someone else unhappy.

An increasing number of states have now passed Canine Good Citizen® legislation and the CGC® program has been adopted by several other countries.

The American Kennel Club encourages all dog owners to participate in this program. You can find out where a test is being given in your area by contacting your local breed club or the AKC directly.

In order to earn his CGC®, your puppy must pass the following tests:

Test 1: Accepting a Friendly Stranger

This demonstrates that your dog will allow a friendly stranger to approach and speak to you in a natural, everyday situation. You and the evaluator will shake hands and exchange pleasantries. Your dog must show no shyness or sign of resentment and must not break his position and approach the evaluator.

Test 2: Sitting Politely for Petting

This test demonstrates your dog's ability to let a friendly stranger touch him while he is out with you. Your dog should sit at your side as the evaluator approaches and pets him on the head or body only. Your dog may stand in place to accept petting and must not show any shyness or resentment.

Test 3: Appearance and Grooming

This practical test demonstrates that your dog will welcome being groomed and examined, and that he will permit a stranger, such as a veterinarian, groomer, or friend of yours, to do so also. It also demonstrates your level of care, concern, and sense of responsibility. The evaluator inspects your dog and combs or brushes him, then lightly examines the ears and each front foot.

Test 4: Walking on a Loose Leash

This test demonstrates that you are in control of the dog. Your dog may be on either side of the handler, whichever you prefer. He must perform a left turn, a right turn, and an about turn, with at least one stop in between and another at the end. Your dog does not have to be perfectly aligned with you and does not need to sit when you stop.

Test 5: Walking Through a Crowd

This test demonstrates that your dog can move about politely in pedestrian traffic and is under control in public places. You and your dog will walk around and pass close to several people (at least three). Your dog may show some interest in the strangers without appearing overexuberant, shy, or resentful. You may talk to the dog and encourage or praise him throughout the test. Your dog should not be straining on the leash.

Test 6: Sit and Down on Command/Staying in Place

This test demonstrates that your dog has had training, will respond to your command to sit and down, and will remain in the place you command him to (sit or down position, whichever you prefer). You may take a reasonable amount of time and use more than one command to make the dog perform the sit and down. When instructed by the evaluator, you must tell your dog to stay and walk forward the length of a 20-foot line. Your dog must remain in place, but may change positions.

Test 7: Coming When Called

This test demonstrates that your dog will come when you call him. You will walk 20 feet away from the dog, then turn to face him and call him to you. You may use encouraging words to get him to come. You may tell your dog to stay or wait, or you may simply walk away, giving no instructions as the evaluator provides mild distractions, such as petting, etc.

Test 8: Reaction to Another Dog

This test demonstrates that your dog can behave politely around other dogs. You and your dog will meet another handler and dog, approach each other from a distance of about ten yards, stop, shake hands and exchange pleasantries, and continue on for about five more yards. The dogs should show no more than a casual interest in one another.

Test 9: Reactions to Distractions

This test demonstrates that your dog is confident when faced with common distracting situations, such as the dropping of a large book or the passing of a jogger in front of the dog. Your dog may express a natural interest and curiosity or appear slightly startled, but should not panic, try to run away, show aggressiveness, or bark.

Puppies learn the ropes of canine behavior from a parent or older dog. If your adult dog has good habits, they will be passed on to your pup.

Test 10: Supervised Separation

This test demonstrates that your dog can be left with a trusted person if necessary and will maintain his training and good manners. Evaluators are encouraged to ask something like, "Would you like me to watch your dog?" and then take hold of the dog's leash. You will then leave your dog's sight for three minutes. Your dog does not have to stay in position, but should not continually bark, whine, or pace unnecessarily, or show anything stronger than mild irritation or nervousness.

EVERYDAY FUN

Not all dog sports have to be organized events. Your puppy will be happy to join you and your family in almost any activity. However, it is important to remember that very young puppies are still growing; their bones are still soft and they may not be fully developed until they are one year of age or older. Hold off on any serious workouts until your puppy has fully matured physically, or it may cause permanent damage.

Dogs thrive on exercise and will be happy to accompany you jogging, walking, or bicycling. As in any form of exercise, make sure your dog is warmed up first and build up his stamina slowly. If you take the proper precautions, your dog can be in the best physical shape of any conditioned athlete, and you will have a great workout companion.

THERAPY DOGS

There is nothing more rewarding than seeing someone else get as much happiness and delight out of your puppy as you do, and there are some dogs that just seem to love getting a smile out of anyone and everyone. Getting involved with therapy work is a wonderful way to spread the joy of dog ownership to those who may most benefit from it. Statistics show that this aspect of health care is making a real impact and creating some remarkable results with the sick, the elderly, and people with special needs. If your puppy has a particularly even and friendly temperament, therapy work may be perfect for him and especially rewarding for you.

You can have your puppy visit the elderly in nursing homes or patients in hospitals, or you can enroll him in a program that helps

The Maltese thrives as a companion animal to senior citizens. His small size and outgoing personality bring a smile to all who meet him.

You and your dog should not be distracted during a training session. He should be focused on you and your commands the entire time.

Praise your Maltese for doing things right. Affection in the form of hugs, kind words, or a new chew toy will reinforce the positive behavior.

educate children about the care and training of dogs. If you contact therapy programs or your local humane society, they can better inform you of programs in your area and the best way to get your puppy started. When your puppy becomes a therapy dog, he is doing more than enriching your life—he is making a valuable contribution to the quality of the life of others.

ASSISTANCE DOGS

Some puppies can be trained to assist people that have physical disabilities. They can help the blind get around independently, help the deaf hear the telephone or the doorbell, and help those confined to wheelchairs accomplish everyday activities, like opening doors or fetching things they need. There are special programs that screen and train these puppies, and some also offer foster programs for people who can take in puppies and train and socialize them until they are ready to be placed with that special person.

SEARCH AND RESCUE DOGS

In almost any city, you will find a search and rescue canine unit. These dedicated handlers and their dogs go to the scenes of disasters and help find survivors and victims. They also help find people who may be lost. They travel great distances and give up much of their time and energy in order to help others—and they do this for the personal sense of satisfaction that they receive, not for money or glory.

It takes a special dog and owner to devote so much of themselves to helping others. Search and rescue dogs come in all different breeds, but all have a few traits in common: athleticism, tracking ability, and perseverance. Getting your dog certified as a search and rescue dog is not easy. You must go through rigorous training exercises under the same conditions that the dog will be facing before you are allowed to actually go to work. The best way to get started is to contact your local law enforcement agency or one of the national associations to see if there are any units in your area. The next time disaster strikes, you and your dog could be helping others—and there is no greater reward of dog ownership.

ORGANIZED DOG SPORTS

Conformation

Everyone thinks that they have a pretty good-looking puppy. If your dog is an AKC-registered purebred and is six months of age or older, you are now ready to jump into the world of dog showing. You may have even purchased your puppy from a breeder with the intention of getting into conformation. In conformation, the main consideration is the dog's overall appearance and structure and how closely he conforms to the standard of the breed.

If you would like to get involved in showing your dog, the first thing you should do is go to dog shows in your area. Spend the day watching not only your breed's judging, but others as well. Judges examine the dogs and place them in accordance to how close each one compares with their mental image of the dog as described in the breed's official standard. These judges are experts in the breed that they are judging. They will examine each dog with their hands to see if the teeth, muscles, bones, and coat texture match the standard. They also examine each dog in profile for general balance and watch each dog move to see how all these features fit together.

There are three types of conformation shows: the specialty, group, and all-breed. Specialty shows are limited to dogs of a specific breed or grouping of breeds. Group shows are limited to dogs from one of

In conformation, your Maltese will be judged against the standard of the breed.

Given the proper training, your Maltese will be a delight to have around.

the seven groups; for example, the All-Terrier Show. All-breed shows are open to all of the breeds that are recognized by the AKC. Most dogs in competition at conformation shows are competing for points toward their championships. It takes 15 points, including 2 majors (wins of 3, 4, or 5 points) under at least 3 different judges to become an AKC Champion of Record, which is indicated by a Ch. before the dog's name.

At one show, a dog can earn from one to five points toward a championship title, depending on the number of males or females actually in competition for the breed.

There are six different regular classes in which dogs may be entered. The following classes are offered to male and female dogs separately in each breed entered at the show. Once the dog is a champion, he or she can compete for Best of Breed without having to win in the other classes.

The classes are as follows:

Puppy Class—Open to 6- to 9- or 9- to 12-month-old dogs that are not yet champions.

Twelve to Eighteen Months—Open to 12- to 18-month-old dogs that are not yet champions.

Novice—Open to dogs that have never won a blue ribbon in any of the other classes or that have won less than three ribbons in the novice class.

Bred by Exhibitor—Open to dogs that have been bred by the same person that is exhibiting them.

American Bred—Open to dogs whose parents were mated in America and that were born in America.

Open—Open to any dog of that breed.

After these classes are judged, all the dogs that won first place in the classes compete again to determine which dog is the best of the winning dogs. This is also done separately for male and female dogs. Only the best male (Winners Dog) and the best female (Winners Bitch) receive championship points. A Reserve Winner award is given in each sex to the runner up. The Winners Dog and the Winners Bitch then go onto compete with the champions for the title of Best of Breed. At the end of the Best of Breed competition, three awards are usually given. Best of Breed is given to the dog judged best in his or her breed category. Best of Winners is given to the dog judged as best between the Winners Dog and the Winners Bitch, and Best of Opposite Sex is given to the best dog that is the opposite sex of the Best of Breed winner.

Only the Best of Breed winners advance to compete in the group competition (each breed falls into one of seven group classifications). Four placements are awarded in each group, but only the first place winner advances to the Best in Show competition.

Dog showing can be a very rewarding experience. But be careful—once bitten by the show bug, many people get addicted!

Once your Maltese has mastered the basic commands, you may proceed to advanced training and trick training.

Junior Showmanship

If your children are interested in training and competing, you may want to get involved in junior showmanship. Junior showmanship evolved as part of the concept that dog shows should be a family sport, as well as entertainment. It was started in the 1930s and has continually grown in participation. It is now an integral part of almost every dog show held in the US and other countries. It is a great way to teach children how to handle, care for, and respect their pets, and also gives them a good start in the sport of dog showing. Participating in junior showmanship is also a great way to foster the relationship between young children and their dogs.

The American Kennel Club rules state that the dog entered in a junior showmanship class must be owned by the junior handler or by one of his relatives or members of his household. Also, every dog entered must be eligible to compete in conformation or obedience, which means the dog must be registered with the AKC. This does not mean that the dog must be of top quality—the rules state that the judges must not judge on the quality of the dog but only on the ability of the junior handler to handle the dog.

The classes are divided into Novice and Open, which are further divided into Novice Junior and Novice Senior, and Open Junior and Open Senior. The Novice Junior class is for boys and girls who are at least 10 but under 14 years of age on the day of the show and who have not won 3 First Place awards in a Novice class at a licensed or member show. The Novice Senior class is for boys and girls who are at least 14 but under 18 years of age and who have not won 3 First Place awards in a Novice class. The Open Junior Class is for boys and girls who are at least 10 but under 14 years of age on the day of the show and who have won 3 First Place awards in a Novice Class. The Open Senior class is for boys and girls who are at least 14 but under 18 years of age on the day of the show and have won 3 First Place awards in a Novice class.

Obedience

You may find that your puppy aced puppy kindergarten and loves to work with you practicing his basic commands. If you have a "workaholic" pup on your hands, obedience may be the right event for you to try.

Obedience trials test your dog's ability to perform a set of exercises. He is then scored on his performance. In each exercise, you must score more than 50 percent of the possible points (ranging from 20 to 40) and get a total score of at least 170 out of a possible 200. Each time your dog gets 170 points, he gets a "leg" toward his title. Three legs and your dog becomes obedience titled. There are three levels at which your dog can earn a title, and each is more difficult

Obedience trials test your Maltese's ability to perform a set of exercises as he works toward an obedience title.

The Maltese's great attitude makes him a natural for conformation and junior showmanship competition.

than the one before it. You may see levels divided into "A" and "B"; "A" classes are for beginners whose dogs have never received titles, while "B" classes are for more experienced handlers.

The three levels are Novice, Open, and Utility, and the dogs that earn their Utility degrees can go on to compete for their UDX (Utility Dog Excellent) or their OTCh. (Obedience Trial Championship).

The first level, Novice, will require your dog to demonstrate the skills required of a good canine companion. He will have to heel both on and off leash at different speeds, come when called, stay with a group of other dogs, and stand for a simple physical exam. If your dog passes, he will earn his CD (Companion Dog) title.

The second level, Open, requires your dog to do many of the same exercises as in the Novice class, but off leash and for longer periods of time. There are also jumping and retrieving tasks. If your dog passes, he will earn his CDX (Companion Dog Excellent) title.

The final level, Utility, consists of more difficult exercises, as well as scent discrimination tasks. If your dog passes, he will earn his UD (Utility Dog) title.

Tracking

All dogs love to use their noses; they use them to communicate with people and other dogs every day. Tracking trials allow dogs to demonstrate their natural abilities to recognize and follow scents.

Even the youngest puppies can benefit from basic obedience training.

Housetraining and Basic Training

This vigorous outdoor activity is especially great for those canine athletes that have an inherent affinity for tracking, like dogs that are in the hound group, although any dog can participate. Unlike obedience, your dog only has to complete one track in order to earn his title.

There are three titles that a dog can earn in tracking events. The first level is called the TD, or Tracking Dog title. A dog can earn his TD by following a track laid down by a human from 30 minutes to 2 hours before. The rules describe certain turns in a 440- to 500-yard track. The second title, TDX, or Tracking Dog Excellent, is earned by following an older (laid down 3 to 5 hours before) and a longer (800 to 1,000 yards) track with more turns while overcoming both physical and scenting obstacles. A dog that has earned his VST, or Variable Surface Tracking title, has demonstrated his ability to track through urban and wilderness settings by successfully following a three- to five-hour-old track that may take him down a street, through buildings, or through other areas devoid of vegetation.

A good way to get your dog started in tracking is to teach him to play hide and seek in the house. Teach him the name of a certain toy that he likes, such as a ball. First, hide the ball, but let him see where you put it. Then tell him to "find" it. After he gets the hang of what he's supposed to do, have someone keep him in another room while you hide the object. You can make the game increasingly difficult by teaching him to find different objects. If he enjoys playing hide and seek, you probably have a natural tracking dog on your hands.

Agility

One of the most popular, fastest growing, and fun events in the US is agility. It was developed and introduced by John Varley and Peter Meanwell in 1978 in England as an entertaining diversion between judgings at a dog show, but was officially recognized as a sport by the AKC in the early '80s. Agility is an exciting sport in which you guide your dog off-lead using verbal commands and hand signals over a series of obstacles on a timed course.

The titles that your dog can earn at an agility trial are Novice Agility Dog (NAD), Open Agility Dog (OAD), Agility Dog Excellent (ADX), and Master Agility Excellent (MAX). In order to acquire an agility title, your dog must earn a qualifying score in his respective class on three separate occasions under two different judges. The MAX title is awarded after the dog earns ten qualifying scores in the Agility Excellent Class.

The only problem with training your puppy to compete in agility is finding the equipment and space for training. Many agility clubs can provide information on getting your puppy started toward an agility title. And even if he doesn't compete, just training for agility can be lots of fun for both you and your dog.

Flyball

Is your puppy an athletic, active dog with a special affinity for tennis balls? If so, flyball may be the right sport for him. Flyball is a relay race between two teams of four dogs and four handlers. Each one of the dogs takes a turn at running over a course that includes four jumps with a flyball box at the end of the course. The dog presses a pedal on the front of a flyball box, which releases a throwing arm that sends a tennis ball up in the air. The dog catches the ball and runs back over the course to the starting line. Then another dog takes his turn. The first team to have four dogs successfully complete the course is declared the winner. It is an exciting sport, and you may find that it allows your puppy to use the right combination of his abilities and turns them into a pastime that's fun for all involved.

Frisbee™

Some dogs just love to play with their Frisbees™; they sleep with them, eat with them, and live to play the next game of fetch. People have taken this natural love and developed a sport that allows dogs to display their amazing athletic aptitude. It all started in the mid-1970s when Alex Stein ran out on the field in the middle of a Dodgers baseball game and performed with his Frisbee™ dog, Ashley Whippet. A nationwide audience got to enjoy the high-flying demonstration on television, and the sport of canine Frisbee™ was born. Both mixed breed and purebred dogs can compete, but dogs that excel in Frisbee™ are the medium-sized, lean, agile dogs that are able to take flying leaps and use their owners as launching pads. Other characteristics that make a good Frisbee™ dog are strong retrieving and tracking instincts, an even temperament, and sound hips.

Frisbee™ competitions are held all over the country. They are divided into beginner and intermediate levels, each consisting of two different events. The first event is called the mini-distance, which is played on a 20-yard field. Competitors are given 60 seconds to make as many throws and catches as possible. The second

Training sessions should be enjoyable for both dog and owner. Make his experiences fun and he will be more likely to obey your commands.

event is the free-flight event, which consists of a choreographed series of acrobatic moves to music. Judges award points on a 1 to 10 scale in each of the following categories: degree of difficulty; execution; leaping agility; and showmanship. Bonus points can be given to competitors with spectacular or innovative free-flight moves.

Friskies and Alpo sponsor over 100 community contests throughout the country each year. There are also seven regional qualifying tournaments culminating in the invitational World Finals in the mall in Washington, DC.

CHAPTER 9

Health Care

INOCULATIONS

Periodic checkups by your veterinarian throughout your puppy's life are good health insurance. Your dog's breeder or previous owner should tell you what inoculations your dog has had and when the next visit to the vet is necessary. You must make certain that your puppy has been vaccinated against the following infectious canine

Your Maltese's health care begins with proper nutrition. Feeding a well-balanced dog food will keep your dog in top health.

Regular visits to your veterinarian will keep your Maltese in good condition.

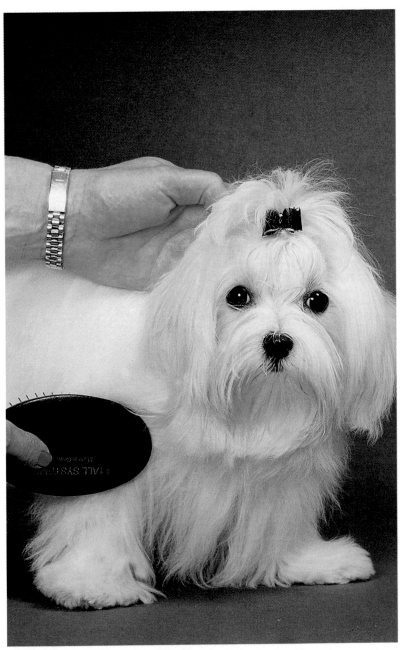

Regular grooming sessions will keep your Maltese looking and feeling his best. Check for any skin problems or parasites while brushing his coat.

diseases: distemper, canine hepatitis, leptospirosis, rabies, parvovirus, and parainfluenza. Annual boosters provide your dog with protection against such serious diseases. Puppies should also be checked for worms at an early age.

DISTEMPER

Young dogs are most susceptible to distemper, although it may affect dogs of all ages. Some signs of the disease are loss of appetite, depression, chills, and fever, as well as a watery discharge from the eyes and nose. Unless treated promptly, the disease goes into advanced stages and can cause infection in the lungs, intestines, and nervous system. Early inoculations in puppyhood should be followed by an annual booster to help protect against this disease.

CANINE HEPATITIS

The signs of hepatitis are drowsiness, loss of appetite, high temperature, and excessive thirst. These signs may be accompanied by swelling of the head, neck, and abdomen. Vomiting may also occur. This disease strikes quickly, and death may occur in only a few

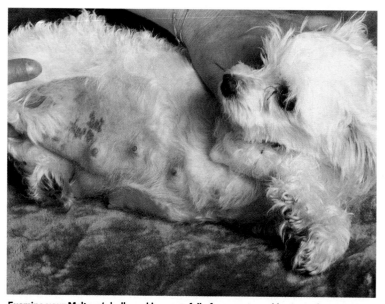

Examine your Maltese's belly and legs carefully for scrapes and bruises when returning from playtime. Also look for burrs or twigs that may become stuck in the pads of the paws.

MALTESE

Maltese love to play outside. When your dog is done playing, examine his coat for ticks and other parasites that may irritate the skin and transmit diseases.

hours. An annual booster shot is needed after the initial series of puppy shots.

LEPTOSPIROSIS

Leptospirosis is caused by either of two serovars, canicola or cope-hageni, and is usually caught because the dog has licked substances contaminated by the urine or feces of infected animals. The signs of leptospirosis are weakness, vomiting, and a yellowish discoloration of the jaws, teeth, and tongue, caused by an inflammation of the kidneys. The frequency of the inoculation is determined by the risk factor involved.

RABIES

Rabies, a disease of the dog's central nervous system, is spread by infectious saliva, which is transmitted by the bite of an infected animal. The dog may show signs of melancholy or depression, then irritation, and finally paralysis. The first period can last from a few hours to several days. After the signs of rabies appear, no cure is possible. The local health department must be notified about any rabid dog, for he is a danger to all who come near him. As with other shots each year, an annual rabies inoculation is very important. In many areas, the administration of rabies vaccines for dogs is required by law.

PARVOVIRUS

Parvovirus is a contagious disease that has spread in almost epidemic proportions throughout certain sections of the United States. It has also appeared in Australia, Canada, and Europe. Canine parvovirus attacks the intestinal tract, white blood cells, and heart muscle. It is believed to spread through dog-to-dog contact, and the specific course of infection seems to come from the fecal matter of infected dogs. Overcoming parvovirus is difficult, for it is capable of existing in the environment for many months under varying conditions and temperatures, and it can be transmitted from place to place on the hair and feet of infected dogs, as well as on the clothes and shoes of people.

A series of shots administered by a veterinarian is the best preventive measure for canine parvovirus.

LYME DISEASE

Known as a bacterial infection, Lyme disease is transmitted by ticks infected with a spirochete known as *Borrelia burgdorferi.* The disease is most often acquired by the parasitic bite of an infected deer tick, *Ixodes dammini.* While the range of symptoms is broad, common warning signs include a rash beginning at the bite and soon extending in a bullseye-targetlike fashion, chills, fever, lack of balance,

Your Maltese can pick up diseases from other dogs, so be careful when out for your daily walk.

Your Maltese needs well-balanced meals and nutritious snacks in order to remain healthy.

lethargy, stiffness, swelling, pain (especially in the joints), heart problems, weak limbs, facial paralysis, and lack of tactile sensation.

Concerned dog owners, especially those living in certain areas of the United States, should contact a veterinarian to discuss Lyme disease. A vaccination has been developed and is routinely administered to puppies twice before the 16th week, then repeated annually.

PARAINFLUENZA

Parainfluenza, or infectious canine tracheobronchitis, is commonly known as "kennel cough." It is highly contagious, affects the upper respiratory system, and is spread through direct or indirect contact with already diseased dogs. It will readily infect dogs of all ages that have not been vaccinated or that were previously infected. While this condition is definitely one of the more serious diseases in dogs, it is self-limiting, usually lasting only two to four weeks. The symptoms are high fever and intense, harsh coughing. As long as your pet sees your veterinarian immediately, the chances for his complete recovery are excellent.

Because this disease is easily spread from dog to dog, it is recommended that your dog get a parainfluenza vaccine before being

A general knowledge of first aid will help you to ensure the safety of your dog in a home emergency.

When you cannot supervise your Maltese, make sure he is secure. Accidents can happen when your dog is allowed to run freely.

kenneled or in situations where he would be surrounded by other dogs.

EXTERNAL PARASITES

A parasite is an organism that lives in or on an organism of another species, known as the host, without contributing to the well-being of the host.

Ticks can cause serious problems for dogs. They are usually found in wooded areas or in fields and attach themselves to animals passing by. They have eight legs and a heavy shield or shell-like covering on their upper surface. The only way to prevent your dog from acquiring ticks is to keep him away from tick-infested areas.

The flea is the single most common cause of skin and coat problems in dogs. There are 11,000 kinds of fleas that can transmit specific disorders like tapeworm and heartworm or transport smaller parasites onto your dog. The common tapeworm, for example, requires the flea as an intermediate host for completion of its life cycle.

A female flea can lay hundreds of eggs and these will become adults in less than three weeks. Depending on temperature and amount of moisture, large numbers of fleas can attack dogs.

Fleas can lurk in crevices and cracks, carpets, and bedding for months, so frequent cleaning of your dog's environment is absolutely essential. If he is infected by other dogs, have him bathed and "dipped," which means that he will be put into water containing a chemical that kills fleas. Your veterinarian will advise which dip to use. Fleas are tenacious and remarkably agile creatures; they have existed since prehistoric times and have been found in arctic as well as tropical climates. Treating your pet for parasites without simultaneously treating the environment is ineffective.

INTERNAL PARASITES

Four common internal parasites that may infect a dog are roundworms, hookworms, whipworms, and tapeworms. The first three can be diagnosed by laboratory examination of the dog's stool, and tapeworms can be seen in the stool or attached to the hair around the anus. When a veterinarian determines what type of worm or worms are present, he then can advise the best treatment.

Roundworms, the dog's most common intestinal parasite, have a life cycle that permits complete eradication by worming twice, ten days apart. The first worming will remove all adults and the second

Everything is exciting and new to a Maltese. Let your dog have many happy and safe experiences.

will destroy all subsequently hatched eggs before they, in turn, can produce more parasites.

A dog in good physical condition is less susceptible to worm infestation. Proper sanitation and a nutritious diet help in preventing worms. One of the best preventive measures is to have clean, dry bedding for the dog, because this diminishes the possibility of reinfection due to flea or tick bites.

Heartworm infestation in dogs is transmitted by mosquitoes. Dogs with this disease tire easily, have difficulty breathing, and lose weight despite a hearty appetite. Administration of preventive medicine throughout the spring, summer, and fall months is advised. A veterinarian must first take a blood sample from the dog to test for the presence of the disease, and if the dog is heartworm-free, pills or liquid medicine can be prescribed to protect against any infestation.

FIRST AID

Just as you would keep a first aid kit handy for minor injuries sustained by members of your family at home, so you should keep a similar kit prepared for your pet.

In case your dog receives an injury, your kit should contain medicated powder, gauze bandages, and adhesive tape. If the cut is deep and bleeding profusely, the bandage should be applied very tightly to help form a clot. A tight bandage should not be kept in place longer than necessary, so take your pet to the veterinarian immediately.

Walking or running on a cut pad prevents the cut from healing. Proper suturing of the cut and regular changing of the bandages should have your pet's wound healed in a week to ten days. A minor cut should be covered with a light bandage so that as much air as possible reaches the wound.

You should also keep some hydrogen peroxide available, as it is useful in cleaning wounds. Cotton applicator swabs are useful for applying ointment or removing debris from the eyes. A pair of tweezers should also be kept handy for removing foreign bodies from the dog's neck, head, or body.

It is also important to take your dog's temperature at the first sign of illness. To do this, you will need a rectal thermometer, which should be lubricated with petroleum jelly. The normal temperature for a dog is between 101° and 102.5°F.

DANGER IN THE HOME

There are numerous household products that can prove fatal if ingested by your pet. These include rat poison, antifreeze, boric acid, hand soap, detergents, insecticides, mothballs, household cleansers, bleaches, de-icers, polishes and disinfectants, paint and varnish removers, acetone, turpentine, and even health and beauty aids if ingested in large enough quantities. A word to the wise should be sufficient: What you would keep locked away from your two-year-old child should also be kept hidden from your pet.

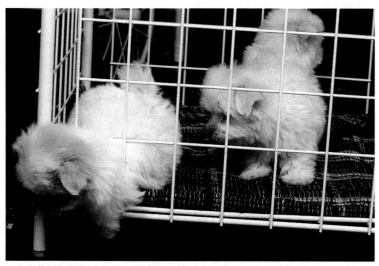

Danger can be present in your home or yard. If your Maltese should have an accident, contact your veterinarian immediately.

There are other dangers lurking within the home among the household plants, some of which are poisonous, even if swallowed in small quantities. There are hundreds of poisonous plants around us, including ivy leaves, cyclamen, lily of the valley, rhododendrons, tulip bulbs, azalea, wisteria, poinsettia leaves, mistletoe, daffodils, delphiniums, foxglove leaves, and jimson weed. Rhubarb leaves, for example, either raw or cooked, can cause death or violent convulsions. Peach, elderberry, and cherry trees can cause cyanide poisoning if their barks are consumed.

There are also many insects that can be dangerous to dogs, such as spiders, bees, wasps, and some flies. A few toads and frogs exude a fluid that can make a dog foam at the mouth—and even kill him— if he bites too hard!

There also have been cases of dogs suffering nicotine poisoning by consuming the contents of full ashtrays. Do not leave nails, staples, pins, or other sharp objects lying around. Likewise, don't let your puppy play with plastic bags, which could suffocate him. Unplug, remove, or cover any electrical cords or wires near your dog. Chewing live wires could lead to severe mouth burns or death. Remember that an ounce of prevention is worth a pound of cure: Keep all potentially dangerous objects out of your pet's reach.

VEHICLE TRAVEL SAFETY

A dog should never be left alone in a car. It takes only a few minutes for the heat to become unbearable in the summer and to drop to freezing in the winter.

A dog traveling in a car or truck should be well behaved. An undisciplined dog can be deadly in a moving vehicle. Allowing him to stick his head out of the window is unwise. The dog may jump out or he may get something in his eye. Some manufacturers sell seat belts and car seats designed for dogs.

Traveling with your dog in the back of your pick-up truck is an unacceptable notion and dangerous to all involved.

PROTECT YOURSELF FIRST

In almost all first aid situations, the dog is in pain. He may indeed be in shock and not appear to be suffering until you move him. Then he may bite your hand or resist being helped at all. If you want to help your dog, help yourself first by tying his mouth closed. To do this, use a piece of strong cloth about four inches wide and three feet long, depending on the size of the dog. Make a loop in the middle of

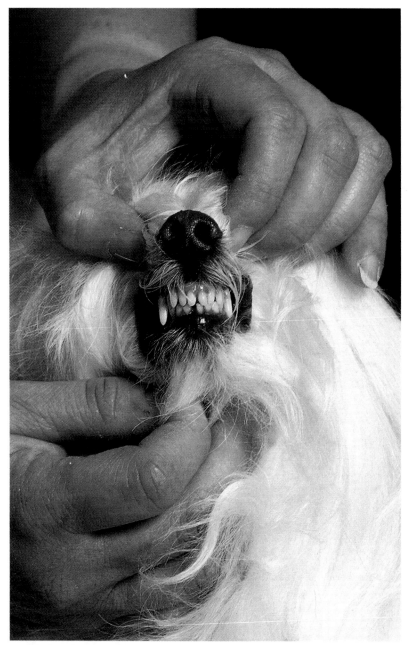

Your Maltese's teeth should be examined periodically. If you notice excessive tartar and plaque buildup, visit your veterinarian to have the dog's teeth professionally cleaned.

Lots of love and proper care will keep your Maltese with you for many happy years.

the strip and slip it over his nose, with the knot under his chin and over the bony part of his nose. Pull it tight and bring the ends back around his head behind the ears and tie it tightly, ending with a bow knot for quick, easy release. Now you can handle the dog safely; however, do not leave the emergency muzzle on any longer than necessary.

ADMINISTERING MEDICINE

When you are giving liquid medicine to your dog, pull the lips away from the side of the mouth, form a lip pocket, and let the liquid trickle past the tongue. Hold his muzzle until he swallows. Never pour liquid medicine while the

Your Maltese will occasionally require medication. Follow your veterinarian's instructions for administering the proper dosage. Sometimes hiding the medication in a treat or meal is the best way to get your dog to take his medicine.

victim's tongue is drawn out, as inhalation pneumonia could result.

Pills are best administered by hiding them in a food treat, such as a piece of cheese or hot dog. The dog will usually gulp down the treat along with the medicine.

ACCIDENTS

It is often difficult to assess a dog's injuries after a road accident. He may appear normal, but there might be internal hemorrhaging. A vital organ could be damaged or ribs broken. Keep the dog as quiet and warm as possible; cover him with blankets or your coat to let his own bodyheat build up. Signs of shock are a rapid and weak pulse, glassy-eyed appearance, subnormal temperature, and slow capillary refill time. To determine if your dog is suffering from slow capillary refill, press firmly against the dog's gums until they turn white. Release and count the number of seconds until the gums return to their normal color. If it is more than two to three seconds, the dog may be going into shock. Failure to return to the reddish pink color indicates that the dog may be in serious trouble and needs immediate assistance.

If artificial respiration is required, first open the dog's mouth and check for obstructions; extend his tongue and examine the pharynx. Clear his mouth and hold slightly open. Mouth-to-mouth resuscitation involves holding the dog's tongue to the bottom of his mouth with one hand and sealing his nostrils with the other while you blow into his mouth. Watch for his chest to rise with each inflation. Repeat every 5–6 seconds, the equivalent of 10–12 breaths a minute.

You need to get your dog to your veterinarian or emergency clinic immediately. Make a stretcher to carry the dog on. To carry a puppy, wrap him in a blanket that has been folded into several thicknesses. If he is in shock, it is better to pick him up by holding one hand under his chest and the other under the hindquarters. This will keep him stretched out.

To maintain his good health, your Maltese should be immunized against contagious diseases.

Maltese are very intelligent dogs that are physically fit and easy to train. You owe it to your dog to take proper care of him.

Your Maltese needs you more than ever as he gets older. The mature dog may need extra care and attention to stay healthy.

Health Care

It is always better to roll an injured dog than to try to lift him. First, apply a muzzle. Then, send someone for a blanket and roll him gently onto it. Two people, one on each side, can make a stretcher out of the blanket and move the dog easily. Try to move him as little as possible.

If no blanket is available and the injured dog must be moved, try to keep him as flat as possible. Get medical assistance for him immediately.

It should be mentioned that car accidents can be avoided if your dog is confined at all times, either indoors or in a fenced-in yard or some other protective enclosure. Never allow your dog to roam free; even a well-trained dog may dart into the street—and the result could be tragic.

Always leash your dog so that he will be protected from moving vehicles.

ILLNESS

It is important to watch for any telltale signs of illness so that you can spare your pet any unnecessary suffering. Your dog's eyes, for example, should normally be bright and alert, so watch for signs of illness or irritation. If your dog has matter in the corners of his eyes, bathe them with a mild eye wash; obtain ointment or eye drops from your veterinarian to treat a chronic condition.

If your dog scratches at his ears or shakes his head, he may have an ear infection. Regular cleaning of the outer ear can help keep your dog's ears clean and free of waxy buildup. If your dog's ears have dirt or dried blood in them, it is indicative of ear mites or infection and should be treated immediately by a vet. Sore ears due to insect bites should be washed with mild soap and water, then covered with a soothing ointment and wrapped in gauze if necessary.

CANINE SENIOR CITIZENS

The processes of aging and gradual degenerative changes start far earlier in a dog than often observed, usually by about seven years of age. Your pet may become less active and may have a poorer appetite with increased thirst. His skin and coat might become dull and dry and his hair may become thin. There is a tendency toward obesity in old age in some breeds, which should be avoided by maintaining a regular exercise program. Remember, also, that your pet will be less able to cope with extreme heat, cold, fatigue, and change in routine.

Check with your veterinarian for special care instructions for your Maltese as he gets older.

There is the possibility that your dog may suffer from hearing or eyesight impairment. Other ailments such as rheumatism, arthritis, kidney infections, heart disease, male prostatism, and hip dysplasia may occur. Of course, all of these require a veterinarian's examination and recommendation of suitable treatment. Care of the teeth is also important in the aging dog. Indeed, the mouth can be a barometer of nutritional health. Degenerating gums, heavy tartar on the teeth, loose teeth, and sore lips are common. The worst of all diseases in old age, however, is neglect. Good care in early life will have its effect on your dog's later years; the nutrition and general health care of his first few years can determine his lifespan and the quality of his life.

DEATH OF A FRIEND

The companionship of pets, not only to children and adults, but particularly to the aged and lonely, cannot be overestimated. Therefore, a dog's grateful owner should do all he can to enhance and prolong the life of his cherished companion. Regular doses of TLC (Tender Loving Care) are the best "medicine" your dog can receive throughout his life.

What can you do, however, for a pet who is so sick or severely injured that he will never recover his normal health? Although one is often extremely reluctant to consider the suggestion, sometimes the kindest and most humane solution is to have your veterinarian put him out of his misery by inducing his death peacefully and painlessly. This process is called euthanasia, a word of Greek derivation meaning "easy or good death." It is usually carried out by having your veterinarian inject a death-inducing drug or an overdose of anesthetic.

Such a decision will probably be a difficult one for you to make, but you need not, in fact, should not, make it alone. Your veterinarian should be your chief adviser, and family and friends can assist in the decision-making process. Your children should not be excluded from this painful time; it would be inadvisable to attempt to "shield" or "protect" them from such events, which are an inevitable part of life. They would suffer even more if, later, they did not understand how or why their beloved pet had died.

By remembering the wonderful times with your pet, by talking about him to family and friends, by remembering him as healthy and full of life, you will eventually cope with your grief. It is perfectly natural to grieve for the loss of such a loyal, affectionate companion who has provided you with so many happy memories. People who do not have pets often fail to realize what a very important part of our lives these animals fill and what a void is created by their absence. Others are more sympathetic and compassionate. You can be assured, however, that if you have chosen a painless, eternal sleep for your pet by "putting him to sleep" (an appropriate euphemism in this case), you have done him a final service as a loving, considerate friend.

CHAPTER 10

Identification

There are several ways of identifying your dog. The old standby is a collar with dog license, rabies, and ID tags. Unfortunately, collars have a way of being separated from dogs and tags fall off. We're not suggesting you shouldn't use a collar and tags. If they stay intact and on the dog, they are the quickest method of identification.

For several years, owners have been tattooing their dogs. Some tattoos use a number with a registry. Herein lies the problem, because

Tattooing and microchipping are great methods of identifying your Maltese if he should ever become lost. Your dog should also wear his collar and ID tags at all times.

Make sure you have a clear, recent photo of your dog in case he becomes lost.

If your Maltese should become lost, contact your neighbors as well as local animal shelters and rescue groups. They can help you locate and retrieve your missing pet.

Make sure your backyard is escape-proof if you allow your Maltese free rein in your yard.

there are several registries to check. If you wish to tattoo your dog, use your social security number. Humane shelters have the means to trace it. It is usually done on the inside of the rear thigh. The area is first shaved and numbed. There is no pain, although some dogs do not like the buzzing sound. Occasionally, tattooing is not legible and needs to be redone.

The newest method of identification is microchipping. The microchip is a computer chip that is no larger than a grain of rice. The veterinarian implants it by injection between the shoulder blades. The dog feels no discomfort. If he becomes lost and is picked up by the humane society, they can trace you by scanning the microchip, which has its own code. Most microchip scanners are friendly to other brands of microchips and their registries. The microchip comes with a dog tag saying the dog is microchipped. It is the safest way of identifying your dog.

MALTESE

FINDING THE LOST DOG

Most people would agree that there would be little worse than losing your dog. Responsible pet owners rarely lose their dogs. They do not let their dogs run free because they don't want harm to come to them. Not only that, but in most, if not all, states there is a leash law.

Beware of fenced-in yards. They can be a hazard. Dogs find ways to escape either over or under fences. Another fast exit is through the gate that perhaps someone left unlocked.

Below is a list that will hopefully be of help to you if your dog becomes lost. Remember, don't give up, keep looking. Your dog is worth your efforts.

1.   Contact your neighbors, and put flyers with a photo on it in their mailboxes. Information you should include would be the dog's name, breed, sex, color, age, source of identification, when your dog was last seen and where, and your name and phone numbers. It may be helpful to say the dog needs medical care. Offer a reward.

2.   Check all local shelters daily. It is also possible for your dog to be picked up away from home and end up in an out-of-the-way shelter. Check these, too. Go in person. It is not enough to call. Most shelters are limited as to the time they can hold dogs before they are put up for adoption or euthanized. There is the possibility that your dog will not make it to the shelter for several days. He could have been wandering or someone may have tried to keep him.

3.   Notify all local veterinarians. Call and send flyers.

4.   Call your breeder. Frequently, breeders are contacted when one of their breed is found.

5.   Contact the rescue group for your breed.

6.   Contact local schools—children may have seen your dog.

7.   Post flyers at the schools, groceries, gas stations, convenience stores, veterinary clinics, groomers, and any other places that will allow them.

8.   Advertise in the newspaper.

9.   Advertise on the radio.

CHAPTER 11

Traveling With Your Pet

Your dog can be trained to become a very good traveler provided you begin training him when he is still young. Unfortunately, your puppy's first ride in the car is likely to be to the veterinarian's office for his first checkup and shots. So, is it any wonder he doesn't look forward to the jangle of your car keys? This can be avoided, however, with a few, simple tricks.

These Maltese pups love to travel together. Make sure your dog is safe when transporting him in your car.

MALTESE

TRIPS BY CAR

Familiarize your pet with your car by taking him to a nearby park or open area where he can run around and enjoy himself. Thus, you will have associated the car with something pleasant. When you place his crate on the back seat of the car, throw a dog biscuit or favorite toy into it to preoccupy him. Never allow your dog to ride uncrated, as there is nothing more dangerous than a playful pup jumping on his owner as he is driving. Your puppy should also keep his head inside a moving car because dust and debris could irritate his eyes and nostrils.

Never park your car and leave your pet in it unattended. It takes only a few moments for the heat or cold to become unbearable or deadly to your dog.

LONG TRIPS

When you prepare for a lengthy trip, make certain that you pack a few essential items for your canine companion: a blanket, a thermos of water, pet food, his food and water dishes, favorite toys, and any necessary medicine.

When traveling with your Maltese, make sure that he is wearing his collar and leash.

Don't make your Maltese beg to go on trips with you. If possible, take him everywhere that you go.

Your Maltese will be grateful to you for the rest of his life if you take care of him properly when traveling.

Traveling With Your Pet

Do not give your pet a heavy meal before the trip, but do ensure that he has a plentiful water supply. This will mean that you will have to break your journey several times so that he can relieve himself, but the rest stops and exercise will probably do you both good.

Several hotel chains in the United States welcome well-behaved pets, but it is always wise to ask about their policies ahead of time when you make your reservations.

With basic training and a little common sense, you and your pet will make excellent traveling companions and benefit from each other's company along the way.

BOARDING YOUR DOG

It may be necessary to board your dog while you are on an extended vacation or business trip. In this event, there are several courses of action one may take. Ask your vet to recommend a qualified pet sitter or kennel. In the United States, kennels that are members of the American Boarding Kennels Association (ABKA) should provide very good care for your pet. The ABKA is a nationwide nonprofit organization established to promote high standards and professionalism in the pet-boarding industry.

Make certain to visit the kennel for an inspection before you board your dog. Examine the facilities, check the cleanliness of the stalls and exercise runs, talk to the owners about any special dietary or medical requirements your dog may have, look at the dogs staying there, and find out if there is a veterinarian on call. Also, make your reservation well in advance, particularly if you plan to be away in the summer months or during the holidays.

While this may be a stressful time for your dog, you can help your pet feel less homesick by taking his bed or favorite toy along. Finally, remember to leave an address or telephone number where you can be reached in case of an emergency.

Resources

American Maltese Association, Inc.
Corres. Secretary:
Barbara W. Miener
2523 N. Starr Street
Tacoma, WA 98403-2940
Web site:
www.americanmaltese.org/

Breeder Contact:
Julie Phillips
3703 SE 17th Avenue
Cape Coral, FL 33904
941-549-4446
Email: juliep@sprintmail.com

Rescue:
American Maltese Association, Inc.
Rescue Coordinator:
Debbie Kirsch
46 Maple Village Court
Bernardsville, NJ 07924

American Kennel Club
Headquarters:
260 Madison Avenue
New York, NY 10016

Operations Center:
5580 Centerview Drive
Raleigh, NC 27606-3390

Customer Services:
Phone: 919-233-9767
Fax: 919-816-3627
Web site: www.akc.org/
Email: info@akc.org

The Kennel Club
1 Clarges Street
Picadilly, London WIY 8AB, England

Canadian Kennel Club
100-89 Skyway Avenue
Etobicoke, Ontario, Canada M9W6R4

United Kennel Club, Inc.
100 E. Kilgore Road
Kalamazoo, MI 49002-5584
616-343-9020
Web site: www.ukcdogs.com

Index

Index

The Publisher wishes to acknowledge the following owners of the dogs in this book: Debbie Burke, Emanuel Comitini, Vivianne Creelman, Kathy DiGiacomo, Lucille M. Dillon, Cherie Eno, Annette Feldblum, Ann Glenn, Claudia Grunstra, Arlene M. Johnson, Debbie Kirsch, Robin Lindemann, Matthew A. Nicosia, Patricia Phillips, Lisa Pollitzer, Bonnie-Jo Puia, Beverly Quilliam, & Christopher Vicari.